CAVENDISH

Personal Injury

Litigation

THIRD EDITION

GORDON EXALL, BARRISTER
ZENITH CHAMBERS, LEEDS

SERIES EDITOR

CM BRAND, SOLICITOR

Cavendish
Publishing
Limited

London • Sydney

Third edition first published in Great Britain 2002 by Cavendish Publishing Limited, The Glass House, Wharton Street, London WC1X 9PX, United Kingdom

Telephone: +44 (0)20 7278 8000   Facsimile: +44 (0)20 7278 8080

Email: info@cavendishpublishing.com

Website: www.cavendishpublishing.com

British Library Cataloguing in Publication Data

Exall, Gordon
Practice notes on personal injury litigation – 3rd ed
1 Personal injuries – England 2 Personal injuries – Wales
I Title II Personal injury litigation
346.4'2'0323

ISBN 1 85941 577 6

Printed and bound in Great Britain

Preface

There were major changes in procedure between the first edition of this book in 1988 and the second in 1992. However, these pale into insignificance compared with the reforms introduced by the Civil Procedure Rules. Major alterations have been made to this work as a result of those Rules. There have also been important developments in the law, not least relating to employer's liability and recoupment. This book has always been an introductory text and aims to give an outline of both law and practice; and I have attempted to retain the introductory theme by resisting the temptation to get embroiled in matters of detail and referring the reader to more specialist works when applicable. Some matters that require special care, and more detailed attention even at this level, are set out in Chapter 12.

I have received considerable assistance in this book from my research assistant Victoria White. There would be an ever greater gap between editions had she not helped.

In the second edition of this book I referred to the encouragement and distraction given by my wife Rosemary and son Jonathan and the need to prevent Jonathan injuring himself. In the intervening period Jonathan has been joined by Thomas, Elizabeth and Benjamin. Needless to say a considerable amount of energy has been spent in preventing this brood from causing personal injury to each other. All of the family continue to give encouragement, all provide distraction in their own unique way. Grateful acknowledgment is made to HMSO for permission to reproduce various Crown copyright materials in the book, and to the Court Service for material reproduced in Chapter 10. The law is stated as at 1 February 2002.

Gordon Exall
Zenith Chambers
10 Park Square, Leeds
1 February 2002

Contents

1 Basic Information

The law on which personal injury actions are based is fundamentally the common law of negligence, but this is overlaid by many different statutes according to the factual context of the claim. Practitioners must be particularly aware of the statutory provisions relating to employer's liability and the fact that strict liability attaches in a large number of circumstances.

1.1 General principles

1.1.1 Negligence

Most personal injury actions are pleaded in negligence. Accordingly, the claimant must show, on the balance of probabilities, the existence of a duty of care owed by the defendant to him and breach of that duty causing him damage which was not too legally remote. Quite often, cases are lost through failure to ensure that all these points are satisfied.

On the duty of care, note that a child born alive but disabled, as a result of an event which affected either parent's ability to have a normal child, will be able to sue if the parent would have been able to do so (s 1 of the Congenital Disabilities (Civil Liability) Act 1976).

The claimant may recover damages for nervous shock, that is, a medically recognised psychiatric disorder, as well as, or in the absence of, physical injuries, if injury by shock is foreseeable (*McLoughlin v O'Brian* [1982] 2 All ER 298; *Attia v British Gas* [1987] 3 WLR 1101; *Allcock v Chief Constable of South Yorkshire* [1991] 3 WLR 1507.

The Crown is generally liable in tort under the Crown Proceedings Act 1947. This now includes injuries to members of the armed forces resulting from their colleagues' negligence during active service (Crown Proceedings Act 1987). Whether the Crown (including bodies such as health authorities) is liable for breach of statutory duty depends on the particular statute concerned.

The duty is only to take reasonable care. The flexibility of the standard is shown by situations such as sporting events, where it may be easier for the defendant to show he or she took reasonable care to avoid harm to players (*Condon v Basi* [1985] 2 All ER 457) and, in the case of children, the standard is adjusted for the child's age (*Gorely v Codd* [1967] 1 WLR 19). Proof of breach of the standard may be helped by the maxim *res ipsa loquitur* if the accident was caused by something under the defendant's control (such as a car) and was something that would not normally happen without negligence (such as the car running into a tree). The court may give the claimant judgment in the absence of contrary evidence, see *Bergin v David Wickes Television Ltd* [1994] PIQR P167. However, the onus of proof remains on the claimant (*Ng Chun Pui v Lee Chuen Tat* [1988] RTR 298).

The basic test of causation is whether the claimant's harm would not have occurred but for the defendant's negligence. However, several causes may satisfy this test. Where they each contribute to the harm but are not each sufficient in themselves, the claimant can sue all the tortfeasors (normally better tactically). Alternatively, the claimant can sue any one of them, leaving that defendant to recover from the other persons at fault a contribution or indemnity for the damages he has paid to the claimant (Civil Liability (Contribution) Act 1978). However, the position is more difficult where each factor might have been sufficient in itself to have caused the injury (see 1.6.2).

For detailed discussion of the law of negligence and torts see *Clerk and Lindsell on Torts* (1995).

1.1.2 Breach of statutory duty

For the claimant to be able to recover compensation it must be shown that the statute is intended to create a right to compensation, that the claimant is within the type of persons that the statute intended to benefit and that the damage was of the type that the statute was intended to guard against. These questions can only be decided in the context of the particular statute.

However, practitioners should be aware that a claim for breach of statutory duty need not necessarily involve 'fault' or 'blame'. The central issue is whether the duty has been breached. If the statute has been breached then liability can be established, even if the injury was not foreseeable.

Causation must also be established as in negligence cases and there are defences of contributory negligence.

1.1.3 Vicarious liability

To hold the employer liable, the person committing the tort must have been employed under a contract of service, not a contract for services, and acting in the course of the employment, that is, on the master's business and not a 'frolic of his own'.

Where there is vicarious liability, the employer and employee are jointly and severally liable to the claimant. Since the employer under the Employers' Liability (Compulsory Insurance) Act 1969 must be insured against third party claims, it is common to sue only the employer, having first obtained an undertaking from the employer's insurers or their solicitors that vicarious liability will not be disputed. The employer will then be entitled to claim an indemnity from the negligent employee, but employers' liability insurers have made a 'gentlemen's agreement' not to pursue these rights in the absence of collusion or wilful misconduct (which is rare).

Similar principles may apply where a chattel (for example, a car) is loaned by the owner to the defendant for the owner's purposes (*Morgans v Launchbury* [1973] AC 127).

In *Lister v Hesley Hall Ltd* [2001] UKHL 22, the House of Lords held that a local authority was vicariously liable for acts of sexual abuse carried out by the warden of a school boarding house. The test was held to be whether the perpetrator's torts were so closely connected with his employment that it would be fair and just to hold the defendant vicariously liable.

1.1.4 Liability for acts of independent contractors

It is normally enough if the defendant has employed apparently competent contractors (*Cassidy v Minister of Health* [1951] 2 KB 343) unless the defendant was under a non-delegable duty to ensure care was taken (see 1.5).

1.2 Road accidents

1.2.1 Substantive law

The usual arguments are over whether the driver's duty of care to other road users has been broken, whether any breach has caused the claimant's loss and as to any contributory negligence by the claimant.

Where the defendant has been convicted of a relevant driving offence, the burden of proof is effectively reversed by s 11 of the Civil Evidence Act 1968. This requires the defendant to show that the conviction was wrong or irrelevant, for example, because the offence of driving with defective brakes was one of strict liability and the defendant had no warning of the brake failure.

The standard expected is that of the reasonably careful and competent qualified driver (*Nettleship v Weston* [1971] 2 QB 691). The driver must anticipate the negligence of others where experience suggests this is common, but can assume that generally other motorists will obey fundamental rules of the road, such as stopping at red traffic lights (*Tremayne v Hill* [1987] RTR 131, CA). Pedestrians also have a duty to take reasonable care (*Fitzgerald v Lane* (1988) 2 All ER 961, HL, 14 July). *The Highway Code* is admissible to show the practice of reasonably careful road users (s 37 of the Road Traffic Act (RTA) 1972).

Where several vehicles are involved it may be very difficult to establish exactly which vehicles did what damage. The court may look at the matter broadly as being one event to avoid these problems (*Fitzgerald v Lane*, above).

1.2.2 Insurance and compensation schemes

Drivers using a motor vehicle on a public road should have insurance against claims by third parties for personal injuries and death (s 151 of the RTA 1988). Judgments for such losses can be enforced against the insurers, even if the insurers were entitled to or have, in fact, avoided the policy, for example, for misrepresentation by their insured. Notice must have been given before or within seven days of taking proceedings (s 151 of the RTA 1988). Enforcement against insurers is also possible if the third party has gone bankrupt or into liquidation (Third Parties (Rights against Insurers) Act 1930).

However, this will not apply if the driver was uninsured, for example, because the policy was allowed to lapse or if, at the time of the accident, the use of the vehicle was not covered by the policy. In this situation, the judgment will have to be enforced against the Motor Insurers Bureau (MIB) under the uninsured driver agreement. Appropriate notification must be given to the MIB and a very strict regime of notification is in place.

If the driver cannot be traced but it is possible to show that the accident was the fault of the untraced driver, a claim can be made to the MIB under the untraced driver agreement. The MIB will instruct a member insurer to investigate the claim, liability and quantum having to be proved in the usual way. There is an appeal by way of arbitration to a QC.

If the accident was the result of a deliberate attempt to injure, the uninsured driver agreement will apply but not the untraced driver agreement. An application to the Criminal Injuries Compensation Authority (CICA) can, however, be made.

Under the insurance policy, the insurers will normally have rights to be informed of any claims against the insured person and to nominate solicitors to deal with those claims. If they pay a claim under the policy, for example, for repairs to their insured's vehicle, they have the right of subrogation, that is, to take proceedings in their insured's name against any other person who may be liable to recover the amount paid.

Uninsured losses, such as any no claims bonus or 'excess' (the first £50 or other agreed part of the claim) will not be recoverable from the claimant's own insurers and will have to be claimed from the defendant as an item of special damage. Insurers may also try to avoid disputes with third parties and their insurers by making 'knock for knock' agreements under which each insurer pays its own insured for his or her losses. However, clients should be warned that these agreements are not legally binding on them and that they may cause them to lose their no claims bonus.

1.3 Dangerous premises

The liability of occupiers to lawful visitors is regulated by the Occupiers' Liability Act 1957. The 'common duty of care' owed to all visitors (s 2(1)) is very similar to the common law of negligence. The degree of care will vary with the type of visitor, so occupiers must expect children to be less careful than adults (s 2(3)(a)). The occupier is entitled to expect that a person in the exercise of his or her calling will guard against any special risks ordinarily incidental to it, but see *Ogwo v Taylor* [1987] 3 WLR 1145, HL.

Finally, where the damage results from the negligence of an independent contractor, the occupier will generally not be liable if reasonable care was taken in selecting and supervising the contractor (*Ferguson v Welsh* [1987] 3 All ER 777, HL).

The liability of occupiers to persons other than lawful visitors, for example, trespassers, is governed by the Occupiers' Liability Act 1984. The occupier will owe a duty to take reasonable care to see that the non-visitor does not suffer injury if the occupier ought to know of the danger and that the non-visitor is likely to be in the vicinity and it is reasonable to expect the non-visitor to be offered some protection.

Landlords will also often owe a duty of reasonable care towards entrants under s 4 of the Defective Premises Act 1972.

The liability of other persons with regard to dangerous premises, for example, independent contractors, builders and architects, is governed by the common law of negligence.

There are numerous statutory provisions dealing with the safety of buildings. Many of these, such as the Guard Dogs Act 1985 and the Fire Precautions Act 1971 and Fire Safety and Safety of Places of Sport Act 1987 are enforceable by criminal law only. However, the Building Act 1980 and building regulations made thereunder are enforceable by actions for damages in tort.

1.4   Dangerous products

A purchaser of a defective product that causes that person injury will normally have a remedy under the sale contract, particularly because of the terms of merchantable quality and reasonable fitness for purpose implied into sales in the course of a business by the Sale of Goods Act 1979. Formerly, where the claimant was not the purchaser, he or she would have had to rely largely on the possibility of showing that the manufacturer was negligent.

However, the Consumer Protection Act (CPA) 1987 (which replaces the much more limited Consumer Safety Act 1978) creates strict liability for defective products (though note the 'state of the art' defence discussed in 1.8.6). Although the claimant may not have had any contract with the defendant, and may be unable to prove that the defendant was at fault, the producers (that is, the manufacturers of the whole or the relevant component of the product), any 'own-branders' who put their name on the product, or the first importers into the EC can be held liable. If none of these are identifiable, the claimant can sue the supplier (s 2).

Products do not include agricultural products that have not undergone an industrial process. A product is defective if its safety is not such as persons generally are entitled to expect, having regard to any warnings given with the product (s 3(1)). Damage includes death, personal injury and loss of or damage to property, excluding the defective product itself, exceeding £275 (s 5(1)). Section 6 of the Congenital Disabilities (Civil Liability) Act 1976 applies.

1.5 Accidents at work

Employers may be liable vicariously for the negligence of other employees acting in the course of their employment, personally for breach of non-delegable common law duties, or for breach of statutory duty. Vicarious liability has already been dealt with in 1.1.3. Finally, apart from holding the employer liable, it may be possible to seek a payment from the State under the Pneumoconiosis etc (Workers' Compensation) Act 1979 in the case of certain prescribed diseases.

1.5.1 Common law duties

The employer owes personal, non-delegable duties to employees (*McDermid v Nash Dredging and Reclamation* [1987] AC 906, HL) to provide safe plant and machinery (s 1(1) of the Employers' Liability (Defective Equipment) Act 1969); to provide a safe place of work; to provide a safe system of work; and to provide a reasonably competent and properly instructed staff. These duties, however, are only to do what is reasonable and employees, too, are expected to take reasonable care for their own safety (*Smith v Scott Bowyers* [1986] IRLR 315, CA).

1.5.2 Statutory duties

As a result of EEC Directives, many accidents at the workplace come within the ambit of one of the following regulations. The most commonly used provisions are the Management of Health and Safety at Work Regulations 1999, the Workplace (Health, Safety and Welfare) (W(HS&W)) Regulations 1992, the Provision and Use of Work Equipment (PUWE) Regulations 1998, the Personal Protective Equipment at Work Regulations 1992 and the Manual Handling Operations Regulations (MHOR) 1992.

The duties most often relevant are:

(a) to ensure that work equipment is maintained in an efficient state, in efficient working order and in good repair (reg 5 of the PUWE). This is an absolute obligation. Even if the equipment is unsafe with no fault at all on the part of the employer, the defendant has breached its obligations, *Stark v The Post Office* [2000] PIQR 105;

(b) to give information and instructions on the use of work equipment (regs 8 and 9 of the PUWE);

(c) to prevent access to dangerous parts of machinery (reg 11 of the PUWE);

(d) to ensure floors, passages and stairs are sound, free from obstruction and not slippery (reg 12 of the W(HS&W));

(e) to avoid manual handling operations which involve a risk of injury, or if that cannot be avoided, to reduce the risk to the lowest level reasonably practicable (reg 4 of the MHOR). This does not just apply to lifting injuries, the MHOR apply to any case involving 'handling' a load.

Where the employer is convicted of breach of the statutes or regulations this can be pleaded in a civil action under s 11 of the Civil Evidence Act 1968.

For further guidance on employer's liability see Munkman, *Employer's Liability;* and Smith, Goddard, Killalea and Randall, *Health and Safety: the Modern Legal Framework.*

1.6   Clinical negligence

The difficulties here relate to the standard of care, causation and evidence. The last is dealt with in Chapter 4. Note also the possibility of obtaining payments from the State under the Vaccine Damage Payments Act 1979.

1.6.1 Standard of care

The doctor's duty is not to cure the patient but to conform to the standard of a reasonably competent person exercising and professing to have that skill. It appears that the standard will be that appropriate to the function that the defendant performs: a houseman will be judged by the standard applicable to a junior doctor and not to a consultant (*Wilsher v Essex AHA* [1987] 3 QB 730, CA). The doctor must keep up to date, but will not be liable if he or she has acted in accordance with a practice accepted as proper by a responsible body of doctors skilled in that area, even if some doctors would have acted differently (*Bolam v Friern Hospital Management Committee* [1952] 2 All ER 118). This applies to all aspects of medicine, including diagnosis, treatment and advice (*Gold v Haringey HA* [1987] 3 All ER 649, CA).

1.6.2 Causation

Negligence will not be actionable if the claimant would have suffered the harm in any event (*Kay v Ayrshire and Arran Health Board* [1987] 2 All ER 417, HL). If the chance of recovery would otherwise have been less than 50%, the defendant's negligence will not be regarded as causing the loss, and no damages can be awarded: the claimant cannot recover a proportion of the damages for the loss of a chance of recovery less than 50% (*Hotson v East Berkshire HA* [1987] 2 All ER 910, HL). If there are several possible causes, the court cannot in the absence of evidence infer that the negligent one was the cause of the loss (*Wilsher v Essex AHA* [1988] All ER 871, HL).

For a practical guide to clinical negligence litigation, see the Legal Action Group's *Guide to Medical Negligence Litigation*.

1.7 Fatal accidents

1.7.1 Law Reform (Miscellaneous Provisions) Act 1934

This provides that, where either party dies, existing causes of action survive against or for the benefit of the estate of the deceased (s 1(4)).

1.7.2 Fatal Accidents Act 1976

This gives the deceased's dependants a cause of action for the loss of their dependency, if the deceased would have had an action had he or she survived, having regard, for example, to any defence that the defendant would have had.

The dependants who can sue are:
(a) spouses, former spouses and cohabitees for the last two years;
(b) parents or grandparents;
(c) children or grandchildren, including any child treated by the deceased as his own and stepchildren – illegitimate children are treated as the children of the mother and reputed father;
(d) brothers, sisters, uncles, aunts or their issue.

These relationships include relationships by marriage and half-blood (s 1).

The action is usually brought by the personal representatives of the deceased, if there is no conflict of interest, in conjunction with the 1934 Act claim, but if no action is started within six months of the deceased's death any dependant can sue on behalf of all the dependants (s 2).

For the measure of damages, see 2.6.

1.8 Defences

Generally, the onus of proof of these defences is on the defendant.

1.8.1 Contributory negligence

The courts can apportion liability where harm has been caused partly by the fault of the defendant and partly by that of the claimant (s 1(1) of the Law Reform (Contributory Negligence) Act 1945).

The defendant must raise the point in the defence. It must be shown that the claimant failed to take reasonable care and that this contributed either to the accident or to the damage, for example, by failing to wear a seat belt (*Froom v Butcher* [1976] QB 286) (25% deduction if the belt would have prevented the injuries, 15% if it would have reduced them) or by accepting a lift knowing the defendant had been drinking (*Owens v Brimmell* [1977] QB 859). It seems that these figures have been unaffected by the requirement in the MotorVehicles (Wearing of Seat Belts) Regulations 1982 that those in the front seats of motor vehicles must wear seat belts; it is uncertain whether the same principles apply to rear seat passengers who fail to wear a seat belt.

A motorcyclist who fails to fasten the chin strap of his helmet can be contributorily negligent; *Capps v Miller* [1989] 2 All ER 333.

The defence is applied in the light of the claimant's age and physical, but not mental, condition. It is less likely to apply in actions for breach of statutory duty which are designed to protect workers from their own carelessness.

The court reduces the claimant's damages to the extent it thinks just and reasonable, having regard to the claimant's share in the responsibility for the damage, assessed in terms of causation (*Fitzgerald v Lane* [1987] 2 All ER 455, CA) or, more commonly, the parties' relative degree of culpability (*Westwood v The Post Office* [1974] AC 1).

1.8.2 *Volenti non fit injuria*

This means a voluntary agreement by the claimant, made with knowledge of the nature and extent of the risk, to absolve the defendant from legal liability for the results of an unreasonable risk of harm.

Because of economic pressures, *volenti* will rarely be available in employers' liability actions (*ICI v Shatwell* [1965] AC 656). Nor, probably, will it apply to accepting lifts from drunken or incompetent drivers (*Dann v Hamilton* [1939] 1 KB 509). Notices in cars that travel is at the passenger's own risk are ineffective (s 148(3) of the RTA 1972). However, the defence may be available to occupiers, at least with regard to non-visitors (*Titchener v British Railways Board* [1983] 3 All ER 770).

The claimant must have had actual knowledge of both the nature and extent of the risk. However, doctors do not have a duty to warn a patient of all the risks of treatment, but only those that a reasonably careful doctor would mention (*Sidaway v Bethlem Royal Hospital Governors* [1985] 1 All ER 643, HL).

The consent needed for the defence to succeed in negligence actions is not to the risk of injury as such, but to the lack of reasonable care that may produce that risk (*Wooldridge v Sumner* [1963] 2 QB 43). Thus, the defence will not often succeed in ordinary negligence cases, however, see *Morris v Murray* (1990) *The Times*, 18 September, CA.

1.8.3 Exclusion clauses

These are now ineffective in relation to liability for death or personal injury to motor vehicle passengers. Further, attempts to exclude such liability arising in the course of a business from negligence are ineffective (s 2(1)of the Unfair Contract Terms Act 1977), though duties stricter than negligence can be excluded. In respect of other losses exclusion is valid only if reasonable (s 2(2)).

1.8.4 Limitation

General

This is a vital point in personal injury cases. Failure by the claimant to issue proceedings within the limitation period and to serve them within a further four months is the single biggest cause of professional negligence claims in civil litigation. It is essential to make a prominent diary and file note of the expiry of these periods and to have a procedure for regularly reviewing all files to check that such dates have not been missed. A master index of such dates, on computer if necessary, is a good back-up.

Limitation must be pleaded by the defendant if it is to be relied on. It is not for the claimant to apply to have the matter dealt with before the action can proceed (*Kennet v Brown* [1998] 2 All ER 600, CA). However, limitation is normally taken as a preliminary point before the substantive issues are tried. The statutes are consolidated in the Limitation Act 1980.

The basic period

In personal injury actions, this is three years from either the date of accrual of the cause of action (that is, when the damage occurs) or, if later, the date of the claimant's knowledge that the injury was significant and attributable to the defendant's breach of duty (s 14(1)). An injury is significant if it would have been reasonable to take proceedings in respect of it (s 14(2)). Knowledge includes that which the claimant could reasonably be expected to acquire himself, or with the help of expert advice (s 14(3)).

Overriding the time bar

The court has the discretion to allow the action to proceed after the expiry of the basic period if it is equitable to do so, having regard to the degree to which the time bar prejudices the claimant and the degree to which overriding it will prejudice the defendant (s 33(1)). The court must look at all the circumstances including the length of and reasons for delay, the effect on the cogency of the evidence and any steps the claimant has taken to obtain expert advice. The discretion is unfettered (*Thompson v Brown Construction Ltd* [1981] 2 All ER 296, HL). However, if the claimant tries to start a second action after starting one within time which has been struck out for want of prosecution, s 33 will not apply (*Walkley v Precision Forgings* [1979] 1 WLR 606, HL). However, it is possible to use s 33 against a second potential defendant if an action against one defendant has been struck out, *Shapland v Palmer* [1999] 3 All ER 50.

Fatal accidents

Under both the 1934 and 1976 Acts, if the deceased died before the expiry of the limitation period, then a three year period runs from the date of death or the date of knowledge of the personal representatives or dependants. When this expires, an application can be made under s 33. If the deceased's limitation period had expired, then the personal representatives or dependants must apply under s 33.

Consumer Protection Act 1987

The usual rules apply with an absolute 10 year 'long stop' (Schedule 1 to the CPA 1987).

Compensation schemes

The time limit is three years from the event giving rise to the injury under both the MIB and CICA schemes. Both will entertain a late application in exceptional circumstances.

Minors and mental patients

Time does not run until the claimant reaches 18, ceases to be of unsound mind or dies, whichever happens first (s 28(1) of the Limitation Act 1980).

1.8.5 Illegality

In some circumstances, the defendant may be able to rely on the maxim that a person cannot profit from his or her own wrong (*Cummings v Grainger* [1977] 1 All ER 104, and see *Pitts v Hunt* [1989] 3 WLR 795).

The CICA may reduce or refuse any award on the ground of the claimant's character, conduct or way of life.

1.8.6 'State of the art'

Under s 4(1)(e) of the CPA 1987 it is a defence if the state of scientific and technical knowledge was not such that a producer of products of the same description as the product in question might be expected to have discovered the defect.

Similarly, the state of knowledge in the industry or profession at the time will be relevant to whether the defendant employer provided a safe system of work, or took such steps as were reasonably practicable under s 29(1) of the Factories Act 1961, or as were practicable under s 157 of the Mines and Quarries Act 1954, or whether a doctor was negligent in not using a new technique.

1.9   Jurisdiction

The jurisdiction of the High Court, and as far as personal injury actions are concerned the county court, is now unlimited both in the amount of claim and in terms of geography. However, if an action is worth less than £50,000 it must be issued in the county court. There is no longer a geographical restriction on the issue of proceedings as an action can be issued in any county court, but can be transferred to the defendant's 'home' court if the court thinks it just to do so.

Key points

1   Most personal injury cases are based in negligence, however, in many cases it is possible to establish liability on the basis of breach of statutory duty.

2   It is possible for someone, particularly an employer, to be vicariously liable for the acts of another.

3   In road traffic and employer's liability cases insurance is compulsory.

4   In cases where the accident occurs in a workplace there are numerous statutory duties which the claimant's adviser must look at and be aware of.

5   An action can be brought on behalf of the estate and/or the dependants in cases where the injuries or negligence has led to death.

6   The burden is on the defendant to prove defences such as contributory negligence or *volenti non fit injuria*.

7   The usual limitation period for personal injury claims is three years. This runs from the date of accident or date of knowledge. If the claimant is a minor then the limitation period runs from his or her 18th birthday.

8   The court has a residual discretion to override the limitation period in many cases.

9   In some cases (relating to aircraft, shipping and accidents abroad), there are different time limits and shorter limitation periods. In these circumstances, great care should be taken.

10 Proceedings for personal injury can be issued in the county court and High Court. If the overall value of the claim is less than £50,000, proceedings must be issued in the county court.

2 Damages and Interest

This chapter will deal with the types of loss for which damages can be claimed in personal injury actions and how the extent of such losses is assessed.

For a more detailed coverage of these topics, see Kemp (1993) *Damages for Personal Injury and Death*.

A major distinction must be made between general damages, that is, those which cannot be precisely quantified in the pleadings and can only be assessed by the judge, and special damages, which can (and must) be quantified and pleaded by the party claiming them.

2.1 Heads of general damages

The claim for damages for pain, suffering and loss of amenity should not be specifically pleaded as a quantifiable amount; it is not appropriate to claim, say, £3,000 for the claimant's broken leg. However, enough information must be given to enable the judge to assess the damages. Thus, the particulars of claim should contain particulars of the claimant's injuries and treatment, any special effect of the injuries on the claimant, the claimant's date of birth and they should refer to the medical report served with the particulars.

The main heads of general damages are pain and suffering, loss of amenities, future loss of earnings and expenses, and loss of earning capacity. This is not, however, an exhaustive list.

2.1.1 Damages for pain and suffering

These cover past and future physical and mental pain and suffering resulting from the injuries and necessary treatment for them. Damages can also be awarded for nervous shock at learning of injuries to others (*McLoughlin v O'Brian* [1983] AC 410). The damages will take account of any suffering to the claimant resulting from the realisation (if any) of a reduced life expectancy (s 1 of the Administration of Justice Act 1982). Normally, one award of damages is made to cover this item and loss of amenities (but see 2.1.2).

The amounts awarded for pain and suffering and loss of amenity increase over the years as the value of money falls. For values of the pound sterling at various dates see Kemp. However, awards should not attempt to predict future inflation (*Wright v British Railways Board* [1983] 2 AC 773). It is therefore important to use case law with caution, particularly since there are fewer reported cases on less serious injuries. However, refer to Kemp and Kemp (*The Quantum of Damages*), *Current Law*, *New Law Journal* or the Lexis or Lawtel file on quantum of damages in personal injuries cases. In larger or complicated cases it is advisable to seek counsel's opinion on quantum.

The most useful starting point is always the Judicial Studies Board Guidelines for the Assessment of General Damages in Personal Injury Cases. These guidelines are used by the courts and, in some instances, they are not appropriate, however, in the vast majority of cases the courts will use the guidelines as a *starting point* for the assessment of damages.

For important observations on the level of damages see the Court of Appeal decision in *Heil v Rankin* [2000] PIQR Q 187. The court introduced an incremental increase on awards of damages over £10,000, with damages being increased by one-third for awards of £150,000 and, hardly at all, for damages at £10,000. Awards under £10,000 were left unchanged.

2.1.2 Damages for loss of amenity

This refers to the extent to which the injuries prevent the claimant taking part in pre-accident activities and will, therefore, be increased if the claimant took part in many sporting or other activities which can no longer be pursued. On this, the prognosis section of the medical report will be vital.

This head of general damages is objective and can, thus, be awarded even though the claimant is unconscious and, thus, feels no pain, preventing damages for pain and suffering from being awarded (*Lim Poh Choo v Camden and Islington AHA* [1980] AC 174).

2.1.3 Future loss of earnings and expenses

These often form the bulk of very large awards of damages. They are estimated by the trial judge who does the following calculation:

multiplier x multiplicand = product

The product is a lump sum representing the current value of the claimant's future loss. In practice, this is taken as the amount needed to buy an annuity yielding the amount of the claimant's annual loss for the period fixed by the court (which because of the uncertainties of life is always less than the claimant's life expectancy).

The multiplicand represents the claimant's net annual loss of earnings and expenses at the date of trial, that is, the estimated future rate of earnings net of tax, national insurance and work expenses (for example, in travelling to work). Account must be taken of future job prospects (obtain a reference from the claimant's employers or teachers) and other factors (though not inflation) which would probably have increased the claimant's current loss of earnings and current expenses, and extra costs such as nursing care.

The multiplier is a conventional figure, fixed by the judge, related to the number of years the claimant would have worked but for the accident. It makes no difference that the claimant will not, in fact, live so long because the accident has shortened his or her life expectancy: a living claimant can recover damages for these 'lost years', although the claimant's estimated living expenses for those years must be deducted (*Pickett v British Rail Engineering* [1980] AC 136).

However, in fixing the multiplier, the judge takes a lower figure than the predicted pre-accident working life expectancy, because of the possibility that the claimant might have died or been made unemployed before the end of that period, and because the claimant is receiving the damages in a lump sum now rather than when they would have been earned. Indeed, the court will assume that the claimant will invest the damages and earn interest (*Auty v NCB* [1985] 1 WLR 784).

There is now a statutory basis for the multiplier. The courts use the Government Actuarial Tables for use in Personal Injury and Fatal Accidents Cases. A return of 2.5% is assumed.

2.1.4 Loss of earning capacity

This covers the situation where instead of, or in addition to, any current loss of earnings, the claimant has been put at a disadvantage on the labour market by the injury in that he or she may lose their job more readily than able-bodied employees, and if this happens, may find it harder to find another job, or such a well paid job. The leading case is *Smith v Manchester Corp* (1974) 17 KIR 1, CA. The amount of such awards is always uncertain and can vary from a nominal amount to substantial awards of two years' loss of earnings or more, depending on the evidence.

2.2   Heads of special damage

These cover earnings already lost at the date of trial and expenses resulting from the accident which have already been incurred at that date.

2.2.1 Past lost earnings

This covers the claimant's net loss (after making the necessary deductions: see 2.4) from the date of the accident to the date of the trial. In the usual case of a claimant in regular salaried employment, it can be calculated by obtaining details of the claimant's earnings for the 26 weeks before the accident (to allow for variations due to illness, holidays etc) net of tax and national insurance, and multiplying this by the number of weeks off work. The claimant should add any pay rises, bonuses and commission which would have been earned. If the claimant is self-employed, the claimant's accounts for the last few years will be needed and expert evidence from accountants may be needed to establish the extent of the loss.

Loss of other fringe benefits, such as free board and lodging or free use of a car, should be added, as should loss of opportunities, for example, of taking part in a professional sporting fixture (*Mulvaine v Joseph* (1968) 112 SJ 927).

2.2.2 Expenses incurred as a result of the accident

These must be reasonable: the claimant must take reasonable steps to mitigate losses. But a wide variety of expenses may be claimable, as follows.

Travel to and from hospital and/or medical examinations

Medical treatment costs which include NHS charges, for example, for prescriptions and spectacles, or the cost of private treatment since there is no obligation to use NHS facilities (s 2(4) of the Law Reform (Personal Injuries) Act 1948).

Special living accommodation or transport

Expert evidence will be needed. If the claimant thus acquires a capital asset, the annual additional costs of such accommodation is taken as 2% of the difference between the capital cost of purchasing that accommodation and the proceeds of sale of the property in which the claimant previously lived (*Roberts v Johnstone* [1989] QB 878).

Extra expenditure of a normal type

For example, the extra cost of clothing and laundry incurred by a disabled claimant (*Povey v Governors of Rydal School* [1970] 1 All ER 841).

Expenses in connection with the damaged vehicle

For example, the loss of any no claims bonus, towing charges, any reduction in the value of the car despite repair, the cost of alternative transport either hired or public.

Loss of clothing, crash helmet etc

Although only the value at the time of the accident, after allowing for depreciation, can be claimed.

Payments to other persons or expenses incurred by them on the claimant's behalf

For example, payments to friends and relatives for helping to care for the claimant, or the expenses of such people visiting the claimant in hospital.

2.3 Interest on damages

2.3.1 Purpose of awarding interest

Interest is meant to compensate the claimant for having to wait for the money. Therefore, if the loss has not yet been incurred, no interest is claimable.

2.3.2 Authority for awarding interest

Interest may be awarded in personal injury cases where the damages do not exceed £200 and, generally, must be awarded where they exceed £200, that is, in the great majority of cases (s 35A of the Supreme Court Act 1981; s 69 of the County Courts Act 1984). These provisions apply both to final judgments concluding the case and to interim judgments, such as judgment on liability with damages and interest to be assessed later. However, the interest only starts to run on the judgment from the date that damages are assessed. These provisions should be referred to when claiming interest in the indorsement of claim on the writ, and when pleading the claim for interest in the statement or particulars of claim (see Chapters 5 and 11).

2.3.3 Guidelines on awarding interest

The 1981 and 1984 Acts leave the period and rate of interest at the discretion of the court. The courts have laid down the following guidelines to cover most cases, though the judge has a discretion not to follow them in appropriate cases. In particular, if one party is guilty of gross delay, the court may increase or reduce the interest rate and/or alter the period for which it is allowed (*Dexter v Courtaulds* [1984] 1 WLR 372). The guidelines are:

> Special damages carry interest at half the average of the special investment account rates for the period from the date of the accident to the date of the trial (*Pickett v British Rail Engineering* [1980] AC 136). The current special investment account rate is 12 1/4 per cent. For details of the rates see Kemp and Kemp at 16-023.

Damages for future loss of earnings and future expenses carry no interest since they have not yet been incurred.

Damages for pain and suffering and loss of amenities normally carry interest at 2% from the date of the service of the writ or summons to the date of the trial (*Wright v British Railways Board* [1983] 2 All ER 698, HL).

If special damages are incurred immediately after the accident or the sum has crystallised at some point prior to trial, then there is a strong argument that damages should run at the full rate from that date onwards and half rate up to that date.

2.4 Deductions in calculating damages

2.4.1 Income tax and other deductions from earnings

Damages and interest for personal injuries are not taxable when received by the claimant. Accordingly, in recoupment cases, income tax at the highest rate applicable to the claimant is deducted when calculating the past and future loss of earnings (*BTC v Gourley* [1956] AC 185). Further, the claimant must give credit for income tax rebates and the receipt of a tax 'holiday', that is, non-payment of tax for a period on the claimant's return to work (*Brayson v Willmott-Breedon* (1976); Kemp and Kemp, 9-010). Obtain the details from the Inland Revenue with the claimant's written consent.

National insurance contributions must also be deducted, as must compulsory superannuation contributions (although the loss of pension rights can be claimed for) (*Dews v NCB* [1986] 3 WLR 227).

2.4.2 Benefit recovery

Benefit recovery is governed by the Social Security (Recovery of Benefits) Act 1997 (the 1997 Act). Benefits are recovered by the Compensation Recovery Unit (CRU). The primary intention is to affect all payments of damages for personal injury by requiring the defendant to investigate, before damages are paid, whether social security benefits listed in the statute have been paid to the claimant over the same period of time as that to which the damages relate. Thus benefit recovery may take place against a damages award no matter what its size.

2.4.3 The relevant period

Section 3 of the 1997 Act defines the period during which benefits may be recovered:

(a) in the case of an accident, the period begins on the day after the accident;

(b) in the case of a disease, the period begins on the day on which the first claim for benefit because of the disease is made.

The period for recovery of benefit ends on the occurrence of one of three cut-off dates:

(a) the day when final compensation is paid – this is accepted by the CRU as being the date on which the cheque leaves the compensator's office;

(b) five years after the day the recovery period began;

(c) the day it is agreed that an earlier compensation payment finally discharged liability. Thus, the cut-off date is the date of the payment of the sum awarded (*Mitchell v Laing* (1998) *The Times*, 28 January) meaning that if the decision is appealed the recovery period will continue until the payment of the sum awarded. The *Mitchell* rule does not, however, apply where there has been a payment into court, in such cases the period for recovery of benefit ends on the day the payment was made, provided that the claimant accepted it within 21 days of receiving notice of it.

2.4.4 The benefits equivalent to heads of damage

The basic aim of the 1997 Act is that there should be a like for like deduction, benefits should only be deducted if they duplicate the award of damages by being paid for purposes which are encompassed in the corresponding head of damage. The heads of damage and the corresponding benefits are listed in Sched 2 to the 1997 Act. The Act divides the heads of damages against which benefits can be recovered into three sections:

(a) loss of earnings;

(b) loss of mobility;

(c) cost of care.

No benefit can be deducted from certain heads of damage, notably from compensation for pain, suffering and loss of amenity. Thus, in extreme cases, the injured person will get some compensation and his award cannot be reduced to nothing. It should also be noted that the 1997 Act requires the compensator to reimburse the State for all recoverable benefits received, even if they cannot be offset fully against the damages.

2.4.5 Recoverable benefits (listed in Sched 2 to the 1997 Act)

- Incapacity benefit
- Income support
- Disability living allowance
- Industrial injuries disablement benefit
- Invalidity benefit

- Severe disablement allowance
- Sickness benefit
- Reduced earnings allowance
- Attendance allowance
- Mobility allowance
- Unemployment benefit.
- Constant attendance allowance
- Disability working allowance
- Jobseekers allowance
- Exceptionally severe disablement allowance

2.4.6 Non recoverable benefits

The benefits which are not listed in the schedule are not recoverable from any award of damages, as the benefits do not have any link with the tortious injury. Therefore, the unlisted benefits which must be left out of account include:

- Child benefit
- Family credit
- Earnings top-up
- Guardians allowance
- Housing benefit
- Invalid care allowance
- Maternity allowance
- Old Cases Act Benefits
- Statutory maternity pay
- Retirement pension
- Retirement allowance
- Social fund payments
- War pensions
- Widows' benefits

2.4.7 How the recoupment system works

By s 23(1) of the 1997 Act, when compensators receive a claim for compensation they must give the Secretary of State certain information about it within 14 days of receiving the claim, as regulated by the Social

Security (Recovery of Benefit) Regulations 1997. This is done by completing and returning form CRU 1. Compensators are required to inform the CRU of the following:

(a) the full name and address of the injured person;

(b) the injured person's date of birth and national insurance number;

(c) the date of the accident or injury;

(d) the nature of the accident or disease;

(d) details of the injured person's employment (if the date of the injury or diagnosis of disease is before 6 April 1994).

The CRU will acknowledge receipt of notification of a claim by sending to the compensator a CRU 4 form. This form must be used again when the case is about to be settled, as it is the form on which application must be made for a Certificate of Recoverable Benefit which governs the amount of benefit required to be repaid.

2.4.8 Obtaining a certificate of recoverable benefit

Before an action is settled, a payment made into court, or payment made under a judgment, the defendant obtains a Certificate of Recoverable Benefit from the DSS CRU. The certificate will detail the amount of the relevant benefits paid to the claimant and the defendant pays this amount direct to the DSS and the balance to the victim or into court as the case may be.

2.5   Fatal accident cases: Law Reform (Miscellaneous Provisions) Act 1934

The claimant's estate can recover reasonable funeral expenses, any special damages the claimant could have claimed, including loss of earnings (if any), from the date of the accident to the date of death, and general damages for pain, suffering and loss of amenity (unless death was instantaneous). However, damages for loss of earnings in the 'lost years' (see 2.4) cannot be claimed (s 4 of the Administration of Justice Act 1982).

2.6   Fatal accident cases: Fatal Accidents Act 1976

The following types of damages may be claimed.

2.6.1   Damages for bereavement

These are currently £7,500 and can be claimed by the spouse of the deceased, or the parents of a deceased unmarried minor (s 1A of the Administration of Justice Act 1982). This is the only non-financial loss that can be claimed.

2.6.2   Loss of dependency on the deceased

This applies where the deceased contributed to the financial support of the claimants. It covers, firstly, the claimants' actual loss to the date of the trial. If the deceased was a minor, this may be little or nothing. Secondly, there can be claimed the estimated future loss. This could be considerable if the deceased was a child to whom the claimants would later have looked for support.

In fixing the appropriate multiplier to reflect the length of the dependency, the court should have regard to the Government Actuarial Tables. The multiplier usually applies from the date of death, although the losses are worked out as at the date of trial. However, the Law Commission has recommended that, in future, the courts, take the multiplier from the date of trial.

In calculating the multiplicand, the annual net loss where the deceased was the main breadwinner, it is usually simplest to take the deceased's net income and deduct a figure to cover the money the deceased spent on him or herself. This will usually be taken as about 33% (that is, 66% dependency) if there are no children, or 25% (that is, 75% dependency) if there are children (*Harris v Empress Motors* [1983] 3 All ER 561). If the deceased was not the main earner, then it is necessary to calculate the net annual loss, taking account of the loss of the deceased's earnings and the cost of providing substitute services, but deducting any financial savings in the cost of food, clothing etc (*Spittle v Bunney* (1988) *The Independent*, 10 February). However, any benefits accruing to the dependants from the deceased's estate are disregarded.

2.6.3 Interest

Damages from the date of death to the date of the trial carry interest. Bereavement damages carry interest at the full rate and there is a strong argument that all losses incurred immediately after the death should carry interest at the full rate. Damages for future loss from the date of the trial carry no interest.

Such damages will be apportioned by the court between the dependants, generally giving the widow the largest share and younger children more than older children. Damages for pain and suffering awarded under the 1934 Act are deducted from the 1976 Act award.

2.6.4 Further reading

For further reading on Fatal Accident damages, see Kemp, Chapter 19, *Fatal Accidents: A Practical Guide* by Michael Yelton, and the *APIL Guide to Fatal Accidents* (Exall).

2.7   Provisional damages

2.7.1 Purpose of provisional damages

Normally, only one award of damages can be made. If the claimant's condition later changes, he or she may turn out to have been under (or over) compensated. The court will try to take account of such possibilities in fixing its award, but often the parties will seek to delay settling the case until the prognosis is clear. Other procedures for reducing delay in providing compensation for the claimant include interim payments of damages (see 6.3) and trying the issues of liability and quantum separately (see 7.1). The new provisional damages procedure is designed to deal with situations where there is a chance that the claimant will develop some serious disease or suffer some serious deterioration in physical or mental condition (s 32A of the Supreme Court Act 1981 and s 51 of the County Courts Act 1984).

2.7.2 When are provisional damages appropriate?

The reference to 'a chance' in s 32A implies that something less than the balance of probabilities is sufficient. Most head injuries, for example, carry some risk of epilepsy, clearly a serious deterioration. In *Willson v Ministry* of Defence [1991] 1 All ER 638, provisional damages were refused in a case where the claimant was going to suffer from osteoarthritis deterioration. It was also said that the courts were concerned with a measurable rather than a fanciful chance.

2.7.3 Provisional damages procedure

1 Claimant specifically pleads provisional damages.

2 (No judgment in default can now be entered.)

(Defendant may request further information in respect of possible deterioration.)

(Defendant may make written offer to submit to an award of provisional damages – similar in effect to a payment into court.)

3 Court makes order for provisional damages after trial or consent summons.

(Possible deterioration/disease and period for application for further award must be stated.)

4 Claimant lodges medical report and other documents at court.

5 If the deterioration occurs. Claimant within period gives three months' notice to defendant and defendant's insurers of intention to seek further award/extension of period and, within 21 days of end of three months, issues and serves summons for directions.

(Court preserves file for period. See [1985] 1 WLR 961.)

6 Directions complied with.

7 Court grants/refuses further award.

See Kemp and Kemp, Chapter 12.

2.8 Damages payable by instalments (structured settlements)

2.8.1 Purpose of the scheme

Damages awarded by the court are payable immediately. However, it may be beneficial to the claimant, particularly one who is severely disabled, say, to receive payment by instalments. Previously, this was effectively prevented by the view of the Inland Revenue that such payments would incur liability to income tax. However, a new (voluntary) scheme which seems to prevent liability to income tax has just been agreed on an extra-statutory basis between the Revenue and the

Association of British Insurers, on the basis that the claim is being satisfied by periodic payments in lieu of a lump sum.

There is a detailed explanation of structured settlements in Kemp, Chapter 6A.

Key points

1 The main heads of general damages are pain and suffering, loss of amenities and future loss of earnings and expenses.

2 Claims can be made for loss of earning capacity if the claimant is at a disadvantage in the labour market.

3 A party can recover interest on damages. It is important that interest be pleaded.

4 State benefits received by the claimant can be deducted from the claimant's award. The benefits are set off against similar awards of damages.

5 In fatal cases, there is a claim, for a limited class of claimants, for bereavement and a claim by the dependents for loss of dependency.

6 A claimant can award provisional damages if there is a chance of serious deterioration.

7 The parties can agree to damages being paid by instalments.

3 Financing the Case

3.1 General principles

You should consider at the outset how the litigation will be financed.

This necessarily entails an understanding of the general principles as to the award of costs and of legal help and its alternatives.

This chapter deals with the general principles relating to costs in personal injury litigation. It then looks at methods of funding cases.

Only an outline of the basic rules is given here. For more detail on costs see Rigby, *Contentious Costs* or Longman's *Costs and Fees Service*.

3.2 Liability for costs between the parties

Since the advent of the Civil Procedure Rules (CPR), it is essential to be alive to the issues relating to costs from the outset of a case. Practice Directions require the successful party to serve with the bill of costs a 'short but adequate written explanation of any agreement between the client and solicitor which affects the costs claimed', a copy of any such agreement must be attached to the court copy of the bill. It is vital that such an agreement is executed at the start of the case.

The court has the power to make a summary assessment of costs immediately after trial in fast track cases and may do so in multitrack cases. It will generally assess the costs of interlocutory hearings during the course of the claim. At the allocation questionnaire and the listing questionnaire, the solicitor is expected to give an accurate assessment of costs expended to date and an estimate of costs of proceeding with the litigation to its conclusion.

3.2.1 The court's discretion

The award of costs is within the discretion of the court. Normally, the loser will be ordered to pay the costs of the winner, although in some cases these will not be the costs of the whole proceedings. By r 44.3(4) and (5), in deciding what order as to costs is to be made, the court is required to take into account matters such as the conduct of the parties (including whether pre-action protocols have been complied with) and the issue of proportionality – that is to say the amount of costs incurred in relation to the value of the claim. The court has a complete discretion as to whether costs are payable and by whom, the amount and when they are to be paid. A fundamental aim of the new rules is to discourage what the court will view as unreasonable and tardy behaviour with costs penalties. An overly adversarial approach risks adverse costs orders, whether or not that party wins the claim. Furthermore, although the general rule that an unsuccessful party will be ordered to pay the costs of the successful party still applies, the CPR encourage the court to consider a range of alternative orders to be made.

3.2.2 The amount of costs

The amount of costs payable by one party to another is limited to the costs of the action (*In Re Gibson's Settlement Trusts* [1981] Ch 179) and these will not include all the work done for the client. The basis on which costs between the parties is ordered is the standard basis, that is, a reasonable amount in respect of all costs reasonably incurred, the benefit of the doubt on questions of reasonableness being given to the paying and not the receiving party.

The more generous indemnity basis will only be awarded in exceptional cases, for example, where the court disapproves strongly of the way the paying party has conducted the case. Costs will be allowed, unless they are an unreasonable amount or have been incurred unreasonably, any doubt being resolved in favour of the receiving party. These rules remain under the CPR but are reformed by r 44.4(1) which provides that the court will not in either case allow costs which have been unreasonably incurred, or unreasonable in amount.

Rule 35.5(4) gives the court an express power to limit the amount a party may recover with regard to expert's fees.

In deciding the amount of costs, the factors to be taken into account are laid down in r 44.5(3) and include:

(a) the conduct of the parties before and during the proceedings;

(b) the efforts made to resolve the dispute (if any);

(c) the value of the claim;

(d) the importance of the matter;

(e) complexity, time and skill involved in the case;

(f) the area where the work was conducted.

3.2.3 Interim applications

These are applications to the court made after the proceedings have begun and before final judgment. In a routine case, the usual order will be costs in the case, that is, the recipient of the costs of that application will be the party who wins the trial. However, where the application has been made necessary by the unreasonable attitude of the other side in, for example, not giving proper discovery or adequate particulars of a pleading, then the solicitor should ask the court to award costs to the client in any event.

The general rule is that, wherever a 'costs in any event' order is made at the conclusion of an interim application, the court should make a summary assessment of costs unless there is good reason not to do so. The assessed costs will be payable within 14 days of the order unless otherwise stated. A summary assessment cannot be made against a party under a legal disability.

3.2.4 Part 36 payments into court and offers to settle

These are two procedures defendants can use in order to put pressure on claimant or third parties to settle the claim. If the claimant rejects a payment into court and, at the trial, recovers less than or the same amount as that paid into court after deducting contributory negligence and ignoring interest accruing after payment in, then costs will be recovered from the defendant up to the time the notice of payment into court was received, but not later costs; indeed, the claimant will be liable to pay the defendant's costs incurred after that date. The defendant can set off these costs against the damages to be paid to the claimant.

Written offers are letters making proposals for settlement which are expressed to be made without prejudice, save that the right is reserved to draw them to the attention of the court on the question of costs. They may be made by a defendant or Part 20 defendant or by a co-defendant with regard to their share of the damages that will be paid to the claimant. Where there are split trials, a party can make an offer to accept liability up to a specified proportion of the amount fixed by the court. Finally, a defendant may offer to submit to an award of provisional damages. There is also a general right to make written offers where a payment into court is not feasible.

3.2.5 Where there are several claimants or defendants

Two or more successful claimants with the same interest will normally recover only the costs of one set of solicitors and counsel, unless the court thinks separate representation was justified. If the claimants fail, then the court will apportion their liability for the defendant's costs.

Co-defendants may be separately represented, but the extra costs will only be allowed if the court thinks separate representation was required (*Harbin v Masterman* [1896] 1 Ch 351). When the claimant has reasonably joined in several defendants, costs are allowed against them all if the claimant succeeds against them all. If the claimant succeeds against only some, he or she will generally have to pay the costs of the successful defendant, but they can be recovered from the unsuccessful defendant (*Bullock v London General Omnibus Co* [1907] 1 KB 264). However, if the claimant is on legal aid, or is of limited means, the losing defendant may be ordered to pay the costs of the successful defendant direct (*Sanderson v Blyth Theatre Co* [1903] 2 KB 533).

3.2.6 Costs against the solicitor

Note that the court has the power to award costs against the party's solicitor who is guilty of misconduct or neglect in the conduct of the proceedings.

Alternatively, or in addition, it can order the solicitor's bill to be disallowed in whole or part.

3.2.7 Types of costs in personal injury cases

Assessed costs

These are scrutinised and approved by the court. This will be the usual position in personal injury cases in the absence of agreement.

Agreed costs

It is desirable for the parties to agree costs to save the expense of a detailed assessment. Most insurers will be reasonable about this.

3.2.8 Conditional fee agreements (see 3.4)

Where the court has assessed solicitor/own client costs either summarily or by way of detailed assessment, the client may apply for assessment either of the base costs, or the success fee, or both. Base costs are assessed under the indemnity principle. The court has the power to reduce the success fee where it considers it to be disproportionate, having regard to all the relevant factors as they would have reasonably appeared to the solicitor to be when the conditional fee agreement was entered into. Relevant factors include the disadvantage caused by the lack of any payments on account, whether the agreement contains a cap on the proportion of damages which can be subject to the success fee and the extent to which the solicitor is liable to pay disbursements.

3.2.9 Costs under the fast track

The costs of fast track trials are fixed as follows.

Value of claim

Amount of fast track costs which the court may award:

- up to £3,000 – £350;
- more than £3,000 but not more than £10,000 – £500;
- exceeding £10,000 – £750;
- the sum of £250 may be awarded where a solicitor attends with counsel, but only if the court considers that attendance was necessary.

3.3 Costs between solicitor and client

3.3.1 Liability for costs

The client, unless in receipt of funding from the Legal Services Commission, is contractually bound to pay the solicitor's proper costs, whether or not the solicitor wins the case and whether or not an order for costs is obtained against the opponent. The position in relation to claims brought under a conditional fee agreement is ambiguous since the indemnity principles still apply. Further, it is not possible to agree to be paid a proportion of any damages recovered, since this would amount to a contingency fee (r 8 of the Solicitors' Practice Rules 1987). The client's liability is to pay solicitor and client costs. It is for the client to show that items or amounts claimed are unreasonable, and unusual steps will be deemed reasonable if the client approved them. The solicitor should, therefore, seek the client's written approval for major items of expenditure and warn the client in the case of unusual items (for example, a road accident simulation by a consulting automobile engineer) that the cost may not be recovered from the opponent.

3.3.2 Duties to the client

Under the Law Society's general standard on information on costs for the individual client (see Appendix C7 of the Guide to Professional Conduct of Solicitors), the solicitor should inform the client as accurately as possible of the likely cost before starting proceedings, giving warning of the difficulties of doing this and explaining when and what items of expenditure are likely to arise. The solicitor should also regularly report the costs position to the client, who should be told that a limit may be imposed on the costs to be incurred on his or her behalf. Finally, it should be pointed out not only that, if the case is lost, the client is likely to have to pay the other side's costs, but also that, even if the case is won, the solicitor will be charging solicitor and client costs, yet is likely to recover only standard basis costs from the other side.

3.4   Conditional fee agreements

The conditional fee agreement is now the usual funding basis for personal injury solicitors. A conditional fee agreements is an arrangements which means that the claimant's solicitor takes the case on the basis that if the claimant wins she will be allowed to charge a success fee, but no fee at all if the claimant loses. The solicitor will be able to charge up to 100% of normal rates. The Conditional Fee Agreement Regulations came into force on the 1 April 2000 on the same date as Pt II of the Access to Justice Act 1999 came into force, which permits the recovery of success fee and insurance premiums from the other side, so removing the need to take part of the client's damages. If the case is lost, the claimant remains liable to pay the defendant's costs. It is often advisable for the claimant to take out an insurance policy.

3.4.1 Success fees

The solicitor needs to have in place a clear risk assessment procedure for taking on conditional fee agreement cases or face the prospect of financial loss. Solicitors must decide whether the risk is worth taking on and what level the success fee should be. To calculate the success fee, an uplift should be calculated and applied to the costs. In *Callery v Gray* (2000) TLR, 18 July, the Court of Appeal held that a firm of solicitors taking an 'overview' in simple road traffic accidents and assessing the risk from the outset of instructions was entitled to put forward a mark up of 20%.

3.4.2 Information to be obtained from the client and given to the client before conditional fee agreements made

Before a conditional fee agreement is made the solicitor should inform the client of certain key matters and, if the client requires, it provide further information or advice about those matters. The matters are:

(a) the circumstances in which a client may be liable to pay the costs of the legal representative;

(b) the circumstances in which the client may seek assessment of the fees and the procedure for doing so;

(c) whether the solicitor considers that the client's risk of incurring liability for costs in respect of the proceedings is insured against in an existing contract of insurance;

(d) whether other methods of financing the case are available and, if so, how they apply to the client;

(e) whether the solicitor considers that any particular method of financing any or all of the costs is appropriate and if he considers a contract of insurance is appropriate, or recommends a particular contract, the reasons for doing so and whether the solicitor has an interest in doing so.

Equally important, the solicitor must check whether or not the client has pre-existing insurance which could cover the proceedings. In *Sarwar v Alam* [2001] EWCA, the Court of Appeal held that there was a duty on a solicitor to invite a client, by means of a standard form letter, to bring to the first interview any relevant motor and household insurance policy, as well as any legal insurance policy the client may have. Further, if the injured person was a passenger, the solicitor should attempt to obtain a copy of the driver's insurance policy to assess whether or not it carried legal insurance. The solicitor was not under a duty to go on a 'treasure hunt' and a careful assessment had to be made of whether any policy was suitable for the action. It was suggested that in small cases (that is, less than £5,000) pre-existing policies would normally be satisfactory.

3.4.3 Contents of conditional fee agreements

A conditional fee agreement which provides for a success fee should:

(a) specify the proceedings to which it relates;

(b) the circumstances in which the solicitor's fees and expenses are payable;

(c) what payment if any is due – if those circumstances only partly occur, on the termination of the agreement and irrespective of whether those circumstances occur;

(d) the amounts which are payable in all the circumstances and cases specified or the method to be used to calculate them and whether the amounts are limited by reference to the damages which may be recovered on behalf of the client;

(e) briefly state the reasons for setting the percentage increase at the level stated in the agreement;

(f) specify how much of the percentage increase relates to the cost of the legal representative of the postponement of the payment of fees and expenses;

(g) the agreement must be signed by the client and the legal representative, except where the agreement is between two legal representatives.

3.4.4 Notifying the other side

Any party who wishes to claim an additional liability in respect of a funding arrangement, that is, conditional fee agreements, must give the other party information about the claim if he is to recover the additional liability, although it is not necessary to specify the amount of additional liability separately nor to state how it is to be calculated until it falls to be assessed. The claimant must give notice of the following matters. That he or she has:

(a) entered into a conditional fee agreement which provides for a success fee, state the date of the agreement, identify the claim to which it relates and include Part 20 claims, if any;

(b) taken out an insurance policy to which s 29 of the Access to Justice Act 1999 applies, state the name of the insurer, the date of the policy and identify the claim to which it relates;

(c) made an arrangement with a body which is prescribed for the purpose of s 30 of the Act, state the name of the body, the date and terms of the undertaking it has given and identify the claim to which it relates.

Where a party has entered into more than one funding arrangement, such as a conditional fee agreement and an insurance policy, a single notice containing the information set out in Form N251 may contain the information about both of them. Where a claimant has entered into a conditional fee agreement before starting proceedings to which it relates, he must file the notice when he issues the claim form.

It is good practice to inform the defendant of the existence of a conditional fee agreement as soon as possible.

Some defendants will ask claimants for details of the risk assessment, mark up and premium paid. This is not information that the defendant is entitled to. Claimants should refuse to disclose this information since it could harm their case and their negotiating position.

3.4.5 Defendant notification

A defendant who has entered into a funding arrangement before filing any document must provide information to the court by filing notice with his first document. A first document may be an acknowledgment of service, a defence or any other document.

3.4.6 Change of situation

Rule 44.15 imposes a duty on a party to give notice of change if the information he has previously given is no longer accurate. To comply, he must file and serve a notice in Form N251. Further notification must be given if the insurance cover is cancelled or if new cover is taken out with a different insurer.

3.5 Community Legal Service

If the nature of the case is suitable for a conditional fee agreement, representation will be refused. Full representation will be refused if:

(a) the prospects of success are unclear;

(b) the prospects of success are borderline and the case does not appear to have a significant wider public interest or be of overwhelming importance to the client;

(c) the prospects of success are poor.

3.5.1 Investigative support

Legal help will only be granted if the prospects of success are uncertain and reasonable costs of investigating the claim to determine the prospects of success are such that:

(a) disbursements (including counsel's fees) exceed £1,000; or

(b) accumulative costs at prescribed rate other than disbursements have reached or are likely to exceed £3,000.

Investigative support will only be granted where damages exceed £5,000. There must be reasonable grounds for believing that when investigative work has been carried out the claim will prove strong enough in terms of prospects of success and cost benefits to proceed privately. Industrial diseases are likely to be the most common type of case qualifying for investigative support.

3.5.2 Expensive cases

These will be referred to the special cases unit according to the code procedure.

Costed case plan

Funding may be refused if the proposals put forward for progressing the litigation, including proposals as to costs, do not appear to the commission to be satisfactory. Where clinical negligence cases are referred under the section for cost benefits ratio specified at criterion 9.3.2, where the prospects of success are moderate, there should be substituted a ratio of 4:1.

3.5.3 Support funding

Litigation support can only be provided where a conditional fee agreement is backed by insurance cover in relation to the other side's costs to ensure that a successful unassisted opponent is not cut off from funds as a result of the case proceeding with litigation support. The insurance cover must be adequate and provide cover of at least £100,000. Litigation support is only available where reasonable costs of litigation, including the cost at the investigative stage, are such that:

(a) disbursements are likely to exceed or have exceeded £5,000;

(b) costs of the case at the prescribed rate excluding disbursements have reached or are likely to exceed £15,000;

(c) for litigation support counsel's fees do not count as disbursements but for litigation funding they do.

Litigation support can only be provided where the prospects of success are at least 50% and support will always be refused if the prospects are unclear or borderline.

Except for cases which have a wider public interest, cases applying for litigation support must also satisfy the strict cost benefit ratio which applies to quantifiable claims under the general funding code. This means that damages must always exceed costs. Support funding can only be carried out by firms authorised by contract to do so. Investigative and litigation support will be administered separately, thus, applications must be made on the appropriate form. Formal application for litigation support should be made only when the threshold has been reached or will shortly be reached.

Solicitors may write to the special cases unit at any time during the case to seek a view as to whether the criteria for support funding is likely to be satisfied. A letter should be accompanied by an application form for litigation support containing all relevant information.

3.5.4 Clinical negligence

A wider range of public funding is available for clinical negligence cases. Funding can only be made for claims where the solicitor has a contract with the Legal Services Commission in clinical negligence which usually means membership of a specialist panel of the Law Society or Action for Victims of Medical Accidents. The general funding code applies, but if mediation is offered and rejected by the claimant it must be justified or funding may be refused or discontinued. If the value of the claim is not likely to exceed £10,000 investigative help may be refused if pursuing the NHS complaints procedure is more appropriate for the client. If an application is made for a claim worth less than £10,000, the solicitor must justify why the complaints procedure is not appropriate. Investigative help may only be granted where investigative work is required to determine the prospects of success. The solicitor should be satisfied on the basis of the limited information available that there is a real possibility that a negligent act or omission has caused the claimant's injury. A formal investigative definition will be given with the initial certificate and, in addition, the solicitor will be limited to £3,500, though this can be varied if justified.

3.6 Alternatives to Community Legal Service funding

3.6.1 Legal expenses insurance

Your client may have a specific legal expenses policy. More likely, the client will have cover under a more general policy such as house contents, a motor policy or a small boat or pet insurance policy. The insurers may, however, have the right to nominate solicitors to deal with claims covered by the policy: check the wording of the particular policy. In *Sarwar v Alam* (above), the Court of Appeal held that there was a specific duty on solicitors to enquire about the existence of such policies. However, in that case, it was held that the policy in question was not suitable and the claimant could recover the cost of the after the event legal expenses policy from the defendant.

3.6.2 Trade unions

These may well provide legal assistance for industrial injury claims, again normally conditional on using a particular firm of solicitors. Many trade union cases will be funded under collective conditional fee agreements.

3.6.3 Interim payments

Although these are discussed in detail at 6.3, it is worth considering applying for an interim payment at the outset of any case where there are substantial injuries and which seem strong on liability. If legal help is granted, such a payment is exempt from the Community Legal Services Commission, and nor will it cause the client's eligibility for legal help to be re-assessed. If, however, there is no legal help, the payment can be used to fund the running of the case.

3.7 Costs and the Motor Insurers' Bureau and Criminal Injuries Compensation Authority

3.7.1 The Motor Insurers Bureau Untraced Driver's Agreement

The Motor Insurers Bureau will pay reasonable costs under the uninsured driver scheme on the normal basis; however, £150 profit costs plus VAT and reasonable disbursements, plus a further £75 for each extra claimant, under the untraced driver scheme.

3.7.2 The Criminal Injuries Compensation Authority

The Authority will not pay applicants' legal costs, but may pay the expenses of the applicant and any witnesses.

3.8 Common problems and their solutions

Problem	Solution
Substantial amount assessed off bill.	Apply for reconsideration of the bill specifying the items complained about. If still dissatisfied seek a review by the judge.
Insurers offer to pay a claim not exceeding £1,000 in full but refuse to pay costs on the ground that it would have been in the small claims track.	Threaten/continue with the claim if for unliquidated damages; until damages assessed impossible to know the amount of damages or costs (*Smith v Springer* [1987] 3 All ER 252, CA).

Key points

1   Financing the litigation should be considered at the outset.

2   The claimant will be liable for costs between the parties once proceedings are issued.

3   The rejection of payments into court or Part 36 offers could have adverse costs consequences for the claimant. These must be explained in detail to the client.

4   There are fixed trial costs on the fast track depending on the amount claimed and/or recovered.

5   There are stringent rules dealing with the information that should be given to the client prior to a conditional fee agreement being entered into and for the contents of a conditional fee agreement.

6   The existence of a conditional fee agreement and insurance policy must be disclosed to the court and the opposing party using Form N251.

7   Limited assistance is available from the Community Legal Service with a wider range of funding available in clinical negligence cases.

8   There are specific duties on the solicitor to enquire into the existence of pre-existing legal insurance policies before entering into an after the event insurance agreement and a conditional fee agreement.

4 Investigating the Claim and the Pre-Action Protocol

This chapter will consider the basic practical steps which will be needed in every personal injury action, up to the stage of deciding to take court proceedings. Some cases will, of course, never go further than this (see Chapter 9).

4.1 Taking instructions

The following vital matters should be attended to at the first meeting with the client.

4.1.1 Conflicts of interest and confirming the client's identity

Check that neither you nor a colleague have been instructed by anyone with an actual or probable conflicting interest in the matter. Otherwise, you may disqualify your firm from acting for either party. Further, you are under a duty to confirm the client's identity by asking for proof.

4.1.2 Financing the case

The client must be informed as soon as possible how the claim is to be financed and of his or her potential liability to costs. Advise the client generally, some conditional fee insurers insist that the conditional fee agreement and the insurance policy is taken out before any steps are taken to investigate the claim. You must check the policy that you intend to use. Further, you must advise the client as to liability for both his or her own and the opponent's costs. See, generally, Chapter 3.

4.1.3 Taking instructions

Many firms now use a standard questionnaire to ensure that important issues are not overlooked (see 4.10). At an early stage, it is prudent to obtain the client's statement.

Allow the client to tell the basic story in his or her own words at the first meeting. However, once the client is at ease and you understand the basic history, you need full details of:

(a) pre-accident work, state of health and lifestyle;

(b) what the client remembers of the accident, details of any witnesses and whether the accident was reported to the police or Health and Safety Executive;

(c) details of the injuries and treatment;

(d) the consequences in terms of time off work, expenses and benefits received, and effect on the client's leisure activities.

Do not worry if some information would be inadmissible in court, but do ensure that the client reads the statement and signs and dates it. This will protect you if the client later changes the story; further, if the client dies or becomes unable to give evidence before the trial, the statement can still go into evidence under the Civil Evidence Acts.

4.1.4 Initial advice

It should be possible in many cases to give the client some idea of the chances of success on liability at the first interview or soon afterwards. It is generally wise, however, to defer any definite advice on the value of the claim until a medical report and information on special damages has been obtained.

4.2 Preliminary correspondence

4.2.1 Contacting witnesses

Interview witnesses and take signed and dated statements from them for the reasons set out above. There is nothing to stop you interviewing someone who has already given a statement to another party: there is no property in a witness. Although other employees, say, may be reluctant to give evidence against the employer, you can remind them that you can, if necessary, compel them to attend court to give evidence (see 8.3.2).

4.2.2 Obtaining reports

If the accident happened on a public road, it should have been reported to the police. The police report will normally be available from the chief constable once any criminal proceedings are completed or the police have decided not to prosecute. The report will contain details of the vehicles, parties and their insurers, the accident scene, a plan and sometimes photographs, the views of the investigating officer as to the cause of the accident and, often, statements by those involved and any witnesses. If the case becomes defended, it is possible to take further statements from the investigating officer on payment of a further fee and submitting the statement to the police for checking.

In the case of industrial accidents, ask to see the employer's accident book and, in the case of major incidents, ask the Health and Safety Executive whether the notification form (Form 2058) has been submitted, and if they can release any statements or photographs.

It may also be advisable to instruct expert witnesses at this stage: see 4.4.

4.2.3 Details of special damages

It will be necessary to write to the claimant's employers for details of pre- and post-accident earnings and of any statutory sick pay received; to the Compensation Recovery Unit for details of state benefits (for address see Chapter 14); and to the claimant's tax office for confirmation of any tax rebates paid.

4.2.4 The letter before action

In a road traffic case, it is prudent for the claimant's solicitor to make a request under s 154 of the Road Traffic Act, that is a specific request for insurance details. It is wise to do this in every case because of the Motor Insurers Bureau (MIB) requirements that this be done as soon as practicable, otherwise a claim cannot be made under the MIB scheme. At the outset, you cannot be sure whether the defendant will be insured or not, if you fail to make an enquiry under s 154 you may not be able to make a claim under the MIB scheme.

Once the claimant's solicitor is satisfied that the claimant has a cause of action, the solicitor should write formally to the defendant (or the defendant's solicitor or insurer). Where a claimant is funding the case on a conditional fee basis, this must notified to the defendants in the preliminary letter.

4.3   Terms of Pre-Action Protocol

(For the Clinical Negligence Protocol see Chapter 12.) For more detail see Hendy, Day, Buchan and Kennedy (2000), Chapter 4.

4.3.1 Aims of the Pre-Action Protocol

The aims of the Protocols are:

(a) to encourage more contact between the parties before the issue of proceedings;

(b) for a better and earlier exchange of information;

(c) for better pre-action investigation by both sides;

(d) to put the parties in a position where they may be able to settle cases fairly and early without litigation; and

(e) to enable proceedings to run to the court's timetable and efficiently, if litigation does become necessary.

The Personal Injury Protocols apply to all fast track personal injury claims, and the spirit of the Protocol is expected to be followed for multitrack claims. Where a practitioner does not use the Protocol, a reason must be given and the court will look at the effect of non-compliance on the other party when deciding whether to impose cost sanctions.

4.3.2 Letter of claim

As soon as sufficient information is available, the letter of claim should be prepared, enough information should be given to allow the insurers broadly to value their risk. The Protocol recommends a standard format be used. Two copies of the letter of claim should be sent to the defendant, one being intended for the defendant's insurers. Best practice will be to identify the insurers as quickly as possible and write to them direct, as well as the defendant.

The letter of claim should:

(a) ask for insurance details;

(b) request that the accompanying letter be forwarded to the insurers;

(c) contain a clear summary of the facts on which the claim is based;

(d) indicate the nature of any injuries suffered and of any financial loss incurred.

After the letter of claim has been sent the defendant has three months and 21 days to investigate the matter and comment on whether liability is accepted or not. The letter of claim does not have any status as a pleading, however, any discrepancies will provide ammunition for cross-examination and costs application, so accuracy is of paramount importance.

The defendant must respond to the letter of claim within 21 days identifying the insurer. If no reply is received, the claim may proceed without risk of costs penalisation.

4.3.3 Disclosure

The letter of claim includes a provision for disclosure of standard documents relevant to the type of incident complained of. If the defendant denies liability, copies of these documents and copies of others in his possession which are clearly relevant to the issues between the parties should be enclosed with the letter of reply. The documents to be disclosed are those which will be likely to be ordered as disclosed by the court, either on an application for pre-action disclosure or on disclosure during the proceedings.

4.3.4 Special damages

The Protocol provides that a schedule of supplementary documents should be submitted as soon as possible:

(a) outline details of special damages should be given in the letter of claim;

(b) a full schedule should be provided if the defendant admits liability or an early interim payment is requested;

(c) if the case is capable of settlement before proceedings because the claimant's prognosis is certain, it is best to provide a full schedule together with medical evidence and a Part 36 offer to settle the claim before proceedings are issued.

4.3.5 Expert evidence

The Protocols envisage the use of expert evidence with the choice of expert being agreed between the parties.

The claimant's lawyer should:

(a) seek medical records;

(b) identify at least one, and preferably two alternative experts in the same specialty;

(c) write to the defendants giving the names of the proposed experts.

The defendant has 14 days to accept, reject or suggest other named experts. If the defendant does not reply or objects to all the experts, then the parties may instruct experts of their own choice and the court will decide, if proceedings are issued, whether either party has acted unreasonably. If the defendant does not object to the expert, he will not be entitled to rely on his own expert evidence unless the claimant agrees, the court directs or the first party is not prepared to disclose the original report.

Written questions

Where an agreed expert is instructed, either party may send to the expert written questions on the report, relevant to the issues, via the first party's solicitors. The expert should send answers to the questions separately and directly to each party.

4.4 Other preliminary steps

4.4.1 Inspecting the accident scene

It is useful for the lawyers involved to have familiarised themselves with the accident site and for photographs and a plan to be drawn up as soon as possible after the accident to capture important features such as skid marks. These should be agreed, if possible, in order that they may be put in evidence at any trial without difficulty.

In accidents at work cases, the inspection may be in the company of the expert(s) instructed by one or both parties, however, it is becoming increasingly difficult to obtain leave to adduce expert evidence at trial and it may be that the lawyers attend with a camera. In any case, it is important to ensure that the inspection keeps to the fact-finding role and does not broaden out into an informal 'arbitration' as to who was to blame.

In factory cases, too, the defendant or the defendant's insurers may be reluctant to allow an inspection. In this case, the claimant's solicitors should threaten, and, if necessary apply to the court under s 52 of the County Courts Act 1984 for an order for inspecting, photographing, preserving, sampling or experimenting with any property which may become involved in later proceedings, for example, the machine alleged to have caused the injuries.

4.4.2 Pre-action discovery

Again in work accident cases, the defendant may have documents, such as safety committee minutes, relating to both the present and perhaps previous similar accidents that may indicate, for example, an unsafe system of work. The defendant may refuse to disclose whether there are such documents until the normal discovery stage after the case has begun.

The claimant may obtain this evidence by pre-action discovery:

(a) the defendant must first be asked to provide the documents voluntarily, usually in the letter of claim;

(b) if the documents are not forthcoming within a reasonable time, an originating summons should be taken out and served with a supporting affidavit.

The court will order production of the documents only where it is satisfied that:

(a) the defendant possesses the documents or they are in his custody or control;

(b) disclosure of the documents is necessary prior to proceedings being issued;

(c) the two parties are likely to become parties in the action.

The statement supporting the application should:

(a) go into some detail about the reasons for anticipating that there is likely to be a claim;

(b) why the documentation is necessary to assist making the decision whether to claim them;

(c) need for urgency if such is the case;

(d) why it is believed that the defendants have the documents in their power, possession or control.

4.4.3 Attending other proceedings

It is important to ascertain the outcome of any criminal proceedings (such as careless driving or breaches of health and safety regulations) against one or both of the parties, since relevant convictions may be admissible in the civil proceedings (see Chapter 8). Further, attendance at such proceedings, and at proceedings such as inquests which have no formal effect on civil proceedings, may give an early idea of the available evidence.

4.5   Instructing expert witnesses

4.5.1 Preliminary matters

An expert medical report will be needed in all personal injury cases. A report from a consulting engineer may be needed in some work accident claims and, very rarely, in some road accident cases. The parties should always be aware that the court will be anxious to limit the use of expert evidence and consider whether it is possible to agree on the use of a joint expert. See, also, the obligations to inform the defendant and agree the choice of expert.

It is wise to check with the expert on the likely amount of the fee. You should also obtain the client's express authority to instruct the expert, in both private and legal aid cases, warn the client where appropriate that the cost may not be recoverable from the defendant.

4.5.2 Instructing doctors

In all but the most trivial cases, a report from a consultant rather than the claimant's general practitioner will be needed. In most cases, where limbs have been broken, the basic report should be from an orthopaedic surgeon. More specialised reports may also be needed, for example, from a neuro-surgeon and, possibly, a clinical psychologist where brain damage is suspected, or from a psychiatrist where personality change is alleged.

Care should be taken to instruct a consultant who understands the demands forensic medical report, and understands the duties that an expert owes to the court.

When instructing the doctor, there is a model set out in the Pre-Action Protocol. Describe the basic history of the accident and enclose the client's statement, in the case of the claimant informing the doctor of the claimant's pre- and post-accident lifestyle. Also, ask the doctor to consider whether the case would be suitable for an award of provisional damages if there is any real risk that the claimant's condition may seriously worsen later. Finally, enclose the claimant's consent for the hospital to disclose their records.

On receiving the report, go through it carefully with the client, unless the doctor has said that any parts of it are not to be communicated to the client. The following terms are commonly found in reports (for more detail see, for example, the *Longman Medical Dictionary* and the diagrams in Kemp and Kemp or Butterworth's Personal Injury Litigation Service):

abduction: moving a limb away from the medial line

adduction: moving a limb towards the medial line

ataxia: loss of control of movement due to sensory defects

avulsion: a tearing

callus: bony material between ends of a fractured bone when healing

cicatrix: scar

Colles' fracture: fracture of wrist across the lower end of the radius

comminuted: bone fractured into several pieces

crepitus: grating of bone against bone or roughened cartilage

dorsiflexion: backward movement

embolism: blockage of small blood vessels

excise: to cut surgically

extension: straightening of a joint

fibrosis: thickening of tissue

flexion: bending of a joint

gluteal: of the buttock

ilium: hip bone

labial: of the lips

lesion: change in functions or texture of organs

lumbar: of the loins

manipulation: movement of a joint to reduce stiffness

node: small knot of tissue

odema: swelling due to build-up of fluid

parietal: referable to the inner walls of a body cavity

plantar: of sole of foot

pleural cavity: space between lungs and inner chest wall

pulmonary: of the lung

reduction: bringing back to normal position

sacrum: five fused vertebrae at base of spine

spondylosis: arthritis of the spine

thorax: of the chest

ulna: inner bone of the forearm

ureter: tubes taking urine from the pelvis to the bladder

Check that the doctor has not discussed the cause of the accident, that there is no substantial disagreement between the doctor's and the claimant's account of the claimant's present condition and for any suggestion by the doctor that the claimant is exaggerating the symptoms. Contact the doctor if there are such disagreements, or points in the report that are not clear (although you must be aware that this correspondence may be disclosed to the court). It is permissible to raise questions of a doctor instructed by the other side.

The defendant's advisers may want a report from a doctor instructed by them. Although they cannot insist on this and will have to persuade the court that such a report is needed, they can seek a stay of the action until the claimant undergoes a medical examination, unless the claimant's objection is a reasonable objection to being examined by a particular doctor, for example, on the ground of a real risk of bias against the claimant. However, the claimant can insist on the following conditions:

(a) the claimant's expenses and any loss of earnings are paid;

(b) no one apart from the defendant's doctor is present;

(c) if the claimant is a minor, his or her parent can also be present;

(d) the doctor will not discuss the causes of the accident.

4.5.3 Instructing engineers

Consider carefully whether an expert's report is necessary. You will have to justify the use of the expert to the court and the court may not admit the evidence or, alternatively, you may not recover the costs. It is essential to instruct an expert in the appropriate field (for example, mechanical or mining engineering) and who has experience of preparing reports for litigation.

Also, give the engineer as much information about the case as possible, although remember that the letter of instruction may have to be disclosed to the court.

Arrange an inspection of the site, and obtain the defendant's undertaking that the relevant features such as the machine allegedly involved should not be altered in the meantime. Ensure that the expert is made clear as to the issues on which advice is required. Check the report when received and ensure that the client understands its implications.

4.6   Negotiations

4.6.1 'Without prejudice' correspondence

Most of these claims, if successful, will ultimately be paid by insurers and will be handled initially by insurance companies' claims departments. It is their usual practice to conduct correspondence, often right up to settlement of the case, on the basis of a denial of liability and under the heading 'without prejudice'.

The effect is to rely on the privilege from production of the letters in the proceedings without the writer's consent, except to prove the making and terms of any settlement reached (*Rush & Tompkins v GLC* [1987] 2 WLR 533, CA). The privilege is attracted by any letter or other communication intended to make concessions or otherwise attempt to reach a settlement of a claim, although it is safer to use the words 'without prejudice' expressly.

4.6.2 Tactics

Advisers of the claimant in personal injury cases should have the central aim to keep up the pressure on their opponent if the defendant fails to comply with the Pre-Action Protocol or to reply to correspondence or denies liability. It is more effective for the claimant to serve the writ or summons quickly, rather than to engage in protracted correspondence.

Once the action is underway, the defendant can put pressure back on the claimant by making a carefully calculated 'without prejudice' offer or payment into court (see 6.1) or by serving a Request for Part 3 Further Information. Both parties should seek to ensure that the case proceeds swiftly. It is not necessarily in the interests of defendants to protract matters (despite the opinion of some insurers to the contrary) since the level of damages constantly increases.

4.6.3 The 'without prejudice' discussion

Insurers or their solicitors will frequently seek to dispose of cases by means of such a discussion at the claimant's offices. It is important that both sides prepare thoroughly for such a meeting, checking the relevant law, the various heads of damage claimed and the current level of interest that would be awarded and of costs incurred. Insurers' claim representatives are likely to be well informed as to the going figure for the type of injuries in question, but there is likely to be scope for argument over the amount of contributory negligence, if any, and of the more speculative heads of damage. The claimant's lawyer should allow the defendant's lawyer to make the first offer. This is unlikely to be the last one, and it may be increased slightly if the claimant's adviser indicates that he or she cannot advise the client to accept it.

Once a definite offer has been made, the claimant's adviser should seek the client's instructions on it, explaining in particular the impact, if any, of the legal aid charge in respect of any costs not recovered from the defendant. Counsel's advice on the reasonableness of the settlement should be taken in cases of substance. The solicitor's oral advice should be confirmed in writing. If the client rejects the offer against the lawyers' advice, a firm warning must be given as to the consequences.

For the procedural steps needed to terminate an action after settlement see Chapter 9.

4.7   Instructing counsel

4.7.1 When to use counsel

Counsel are frequently instructed to advise on liability and quantum of damages at the outset of a personal injury action. Such advice is usually in writing, a conference being reserved until a trial is in prospect. However, in difficult cases where the success of the party's case may depend, for example, on the party's credibility as a witness, it is helpful to have a conference and, perhaps, advice on evidence, at an earlier stage. Counsel will therefore be aware of the case when asked to draft the pleadings, and the client will be more confident that the case is being handled by someone who is familiar with it and whom he or she has met before the trial.

An added advantage for the solicitor is that, if the case goes wrong through the action of counsel, the solicitor should be immune from liability in negligence, provided competent counsel was instructed and competently briefed (*In Re A (A Minor)* (1988) NLJ, 18 March, CA). The choice of counsel is very important and you should take care to ensure that you instruct someone who practises predominantly in personal injury litigation. You should take particular care to instruct more specialist counsel in complex factory or medical negligence cases.

4.7.2 How to instruct counsel

Instructions should enclose all the relevant documents including the statements of the client and any witnesses, the police or Health and Safety Executive's and engineer's reports, the medical report(s), a calculation of special damage, any legal aid certificate and relevant correspondence with the other side. If the matter is funded on a conditional fee basis, a copy of the conditional fee agreement should be enclosed. Instructions should not merely be a back sheet enclosing all the papers, but be self-contained and self-explanatory, outlining the facts and the available evidence and specifying what counsel is being asked to do. This will minimise the difficulties if another counsel has to take over the case at a later date.

Once received, counsel's advice should be discussed with the client and its implications explained.

4.8 The decision to issue proceedings

4.8.1 To sue or not to sue?

The decision must obviously be the client's, but should be made with the benefit of the solicitor's and, where necessary, counsel's advice, both oral and written. In particular, the risks of costs must be considered in both private and legally aided cases, since legal aid contributions are now payable for the duration of a case. On the other hand, it may be essential to start proceedings because the limitation period is about to expire, or it may be desirable to do so to put pressure on the defendant to settle.

4.8.2 Where to issue proceedings

Both the High Court and the county court now have unlimited jurisdiction in personal injury actions, however, all personal injury actions for less than £50,000 must be issued in the county court. In deciding the value of the action for the purpose of issuing proceedings:

(a) no account is taken of any possible finding of contributory negligence – except if contributory negligence is admitted;

(b) where the claimant seeks provisional damages, no account is taken of the possibility of a future application for further damages;

(c) interest and costs are disregarded;

(d) sums liable to recoupment are taken into account.

If the claimant issues in the High Court when the action does not exceed £50,000, he risks having his costs reduced on any taxation of the action or having the case struck out.

There are no longer any geographical restrictions on the issue of an action and proceedings can be issued in any county court. However, the action can be transferred to another county court for reasons of convenience or if the court thinks it best to be in a court near the accident scene.

4.9   Common problems and their solutions

Problem	Solution
Potential witnesses refuse to give statement.	Visit witnesses at home; point out that damages will be paid by insurers; threaten to summons them to give evidence at trial.
Insurers refuse to deal with claim because insured has not reported accident to them as required by the policy.	Point out that such policy conditions do not affect the insurers' duty to pay any judgment against their insured under s 151 of the Road Traffic Act 1988.

Facilities for inspecting factory accident site refused or hospital refuses to disclose treatment records in medical negligence case.

Threaten/apply for orders for pre-action inspection or discovery of documents.

Defendants will not increase their first offer.

Make realistic Part 36 offer in response, prior to issue and thereafter write stating that proceedings will be started unless the defendant's offer is increased.

4.10 Client questionnaire checklist

General information

(1) Full name

(2) Litigation friend's full name (if appropriate)

(3) Address of client (and/or litigation friend)

(4) Telephone number

(5) Date of birth

(6) National insurance number

(7) Marital status

(8) Date and time of accident

(9) Place of accident

(10) Employer's name and address

(11) Occupation

(12) Accountant's name and address (self-employed claimant)

(13) Client registered for VAT?

(14) Funding – member of motoring organisation/legal expenses insurance company is there any insurance available from other sources, or example, home policy or motor policy

(15) Funding – eligibility for Community Legal Service?

(16) Funding – private/payment on account/payment for disbursements?

(17) Funding – CFA appropriate?

(18) Circumstances of the accident

(19) Names and addresses of any witnesses

4.11 Letter of claim checklist

The letter of claim should contain:

(1)   Clear summary of the facts on which the claim is based

(2)   An indication of the nature of any injuries suffered and financial loss incurred

(3)   Details of client's employment , loss of earnings and any other losses

(4)   If police report obtained, an offer to provide a copy if the defendant pays half the fee for obtaining it

(5)   List of documents the defendant is expected to disclose

(6)   Details of the insurer should be asked for

(7)   The defendant must be told that the letter begins a timetable and that acknowledgement of receipt of letter must be within 21 days

(8)   The letter must be sent in duplicate and the defendant requested to send a copy to his insurers or if the insurers are known a copy to be sent to them

Key points

1   Consider funding the case and potential conflicts of interest at the outset.

2   It is crucial that the terms of the Pre-Action Protocol are complied with as far as possible.

3   If acting for the claimant, ensure that a letter of claim complying with the Protocol is sent out as soon as possible.

4   Ensure that experts, particularly doctors, are instructed in accordance with the provisions of the Protocol.

5   It is prudent to have some type of questionnaire/checklist for taking instructions in initial circumstances.

5 Starting Proceedings and Drafting Statements of Case

This chapter deals with the basic mechanics of starting court proceedings in personal injury cases and the basic principles of drafting the necessary pleadings. For more detail see O'Hare and Hill, *Civil Litigation* and Pritchard, *Personal Injury Litigation*.

5.1 General requirements

The claim form (see precedent)

There is a single claim form which can be used for one or more defendants and can contain the particulars of claim. If the particulars of claim are not served with the form, the claimant must file a copy of the claim form within seven days of service on the defendant. The claim form must be served within four months (six months if serving out of the jurisdiction).

5.1.1 Date of issue

Proceedings are started when the claim form is issued. However, the claim is actually brought when the completed form is received by the court, for the purposes of the Limitation Act 1980.

Contents of the claim form

The claim form must contain a concise statement of the nature of the claim, specify the remedy sought, contain a statement of value and give details of whether any of the parties are acting in a representative capacity. If the particulars of claim are not served with the claim form, the claimant must state on the form that the particulars will follow. It should be noted that there is no penalty if a form of relief is not claimed on the form. Under the new rules, the court can grant any remedy to which the claimant is entitled, irrespective of whether it is specified in the claim form, the defendant may have an argument as to costs if he is suddenly forced to consider a remedy not mentioned prior to the trial. It remains essential, however, that matters such as a claim for provisional damages are specifically pleaded.

The claim form must state the amount claimed or that the claimant expects to recover: not more than £5,000, between £5,000 and £15,000 or more than £15,000. If it is not possible to state the amount to be recovered, this fact should be stated on the form. The claim form must state whether or not the claim for damages for personal injury (that is, the claim for damages for pain, suffering and loss of amenity) exceeds £1,000.

As the claim form is a statement of case, it should be accompanied by a statement of truth.

Where the claimant is a child or a person under a disability, the name should be followed by '(a child) by ... his litigation friend'.

5.2   Drafting the particulars of claim

5.2.1 Use of counsel

It is normally best to instruct counsel to draft the particulars of claim.

5.2.2 Principles of drafting the statement of case

The particulars of claim must succinctly state the facts on which the claim is based. They must also state, with grounds, any claim for aggravated, exemplary or provisional damages.

The particulars of claim must include:

(a) the claimant's date of birth and an outline of his injuries;

(b) where provisional damages are claimed, details must be given setting out the statutory basis for the claim and the nature of the deterioration.

Annexed to the particulars of claim should be:

(a) a schedule of past and future loss;

(b) a medical report, if medical evidence is to be relied upon.

Other matters to set out in the particulars of claim

Any relevant convictions of the defendant, stating the date, court convicting and the nature of the conviction and its relevance to the proceedings (s 11 of the Civil Evidence Act 1968).

Where the claimant seeks to rely on the following matters, they must be set out in the particulars of claim:

(a) any allegation of fraud;

(b) the fact of any illegality;

(c) details of any misrepresentation;

(d) details of all breaches of trust;

(e) notice or knowledge of a fact;

(f) details of unsoundness of mind or undue influence;

(g) details of wilful default;

(h) any facts relating to mitigation of loss or damage.

The particulars of claim must be accompanied by a statement of truth and must display the case number, title of proceedings and the claimant's address for service.

Statement of truth

This consists of a statement that the party presenting the claim believes the facts to be true. It must be signed by the party or his solicitor.

Claim for interest

If the claim is also for interest, the particulars of claim must state the grounds on which this is being claimed. In a claim for a specific sum of money, the percentage rate must be stated, as well as the date from which interest is claimed, the amount calculated and the subsequent daily rate.

Fatal accident claims

The particulars of claim must state the claim is brought under the Fatal Accidents Act 1976 and detail the dependants on whose part the claim is brought and the nature of their claim.

Optional inclusions in the particulars of claim

These comprise: points of law which may be relied on, names of witnesses and supporting documents such as expert reports.

Service

Once issued, the claim, along with forms for the defendant to use for admitting or defending the claim and acknowledging the service, must be served within four months. If a solicitor has been nominated to accept service, then service *must* take place on the nominated solicitor, service on the defendant after a solicitor has been nominated is not good service. Similarly, service on an insurance company is not good service.

Ensuring that service takes place on the appropriate person, at the appropriate address and within the appropriate time period is of critical importance. These are not matters that should be delegated.

5.3   Responding to a claim

5.3.1 The defendant's options

Under the Civil Procedure Rules, a defendant has a number of options when served with a claim form:

(a) he can serve an admission in accordance with Pt 14;

(b) he can serve a defence in accordance with Pt 19;

(c) he can serve a defence and a partial admission;

(d) he can file an acknowledgment of service.

5.3.2 Acknowledgment of service

This can be served in two circumstances:

1   where the defendant cannot file a defence within 14 days of service of particulars of claim – filing an acknowledgment effectively gives the defendant an extra 14 days (the time for service of defence then being 28 days after service);

2   where a defendant wishes to dispute the court's jurisdiction.

Content

The defendant's name should be set out in full and his address for service must be given.

The acknowledgment should be signed either by the defendant or by his legal representative.

Withdrawal

An acknowledgment of service may only be withdrawn or amended with the court's permission.

Admission

A party may admit the whole or part of a claim by giving written notice. Where the claim is not for money, only the claimant may apply for judgment. Such a judgment will be that which appears to the court to be warranted by the admission.

5.3.3 Defence

Drafting the defence and/or counterclaim

1   The defendant in his defence must state which of the allegations he denies, which he is unable to admit or deny but which he requires the claimant to prove and which allegations he admits.

2   Where the defendant admits an allegation, the defence must state the reasons for doing so and, if he intends to put forward a different version of events to the claimant, he must state his own version.

3   In the case of a defendant who fails to deal with the allegation, but has set out in his defence the nature of his case regarding the issue to which the allegation is relevant, it shall be taken to be required that the allegation be proved by the claimant.

When the particulars of claim are accompanied by a medical report the defendant must state in the defence whether he agrees, disputes or neither agrees nor disputes but has no knowledge of the matter set out in the medical report.

Where the defendant disputes any part of the medical report, his reasons for doing so must be set out in the defence.

If the defendant has obtained his own medical report on which the defence intends to rely the report must be attached to the defence.

Responding to a schedule of loss

When a schedule of loss accompanies the claim form the defendant should include in the defence a counter-schedule stating which items he agrees, disputes or neither agrees nor disputes but has no knowledge of. When any item is disputed the defence should include an alternative figure where appropriate.

Statement of value

It is a mandatory requirement that the claimant provide such a statement. When the defence disputes that statement, it must state why and give its own statement of value.

If the defence is relying on a limitation period, the defence must set out the details of the expiry of the limitation period. A general assertion that the action is statute barred is not sufficient.

The defence must be verified by a statement of truth.

Counterclaims

The defendant makes a counterclaim against the claimant by filing the particulars of the counterclaim. The court's permission is not required where the counterclaim is served with the defence. A counterclaim my be filed at any other time with the court's permission.

Any counterclaim should be in the same document, immediately after the defence. If it relates to the same incident, it is usually sufficient to refer back to the allegations in the defence. Otherwise, the negligence or other wrong by the claimant must be alleged and particulars given.

The defendant must allege that the claimant's wrongful act has caused loss and give particulars of such loss.

The defendant claims interest on damages under s 69 of the County Courts Act 1984.

Prayer for damages and interest under the relevant statutory provision

The following must be specifically pleaded:

(a) contributory negligence;

(b) denials that the defendant has been convicted as alleged or allegations that the conviction is irrelevant or erroneous.

5.4   Reply and/or defence to counterclaim

5.4.1 Are they necessary?

It is never mandatory to serve a reply since the plaintiff is deemed to deny allegations in the defence. However, a reply is desirable to deal with points not covered in the statement of claim, for example, contributory negligence.

A claimant who files a reply to a defence but fails to deal with the matter raised in the defence shall be taken to require that matter to be proved.

The reply must be verified by a statement of truth.

Pleadings may still be filed after the reply but to do this the permission of the court must be obtained.

Defence to counterclaim

However, a defence to counterclaim should be filed to prevent the defendant applying for judgment on the counterclaim.

5.4.2 Notice to insurers

If the claimant is insured, the insurers should be notified of any counterclaim or they might be able to repudiate liability to meet it. They should also be asked if they wish the claimant's solicitors to act for them on the counterclaim.

Key points

1 When issuing proceedings the proper claim form must be used. This must be served within four months of issue.
2 The claims form and the particulars of claim must be supported by a statement of truth.
3 The claim for interest must be fully set out.
4 It is of crucial importance that the proceedings be served at the proper address, proceedings must be served on a solicitor if the defendant has nominated a solicitor for service.
5 A defendant can respond to a claim by initially serving an acknowledgment of service and then a defence.
6 The defendant should state in the defence what is admitted, denied or what the defendant can neither admit or deny. The defendant should also state what items are disputed in the claimant's schedule of damages.

6 Payments into Court, Part 20 Proceedings, Interim Payments

This chapter will deal with three major defence tactics: payments into court, Part 20 proceedings, and the important claimant's tactic of interim payments. For more detail, see Pritchard *et al*, *Personal Injury Litigation* (2002) and O'Hare and Hill, *Civil Litigation* (2001).

6.1 Payments into court (Part 36)

6.1.1 The purpose of Part 36 payments into court

It can be unfair to defendants to have actions hanging over them which are not of their choosing and which may have little merit. To counter the powerful weapon of a writ or summons, the defendant may, at any time after the commencement of proceedings but before judgment, without admitting liability make a Part 36 payment or offer into court in satisfaction of the claim.

Where the claim includes both a money claim and a non-money claim and the defendant wishes to make an offer which is effective under the rules, he must make a Part 36 payment in relation to the money claim and a Part 36 offer in relation to the non-money claim. However, these rules do not apply to the small claims track unless the court specifies otherwise.

There are two exceptions to the rule that an offer by the defendant to settle a money claim must be accompanied by a Part 36 payment. The first is that a defendant may make a Part 36 offer limited to accepting liability up to a specified proportion. Secondly a defendant can make a Part 36 offer to settle the claim if, at the time he makes the offer, he has applied for but not received a certificate of total benefit and he makes a Part 36 payment not more than seven days after he receives the certificate.

6.1.2 The claimant's Part 36 offer to settle

Furthermore, a claimant may make a Part 36 offer to settle. An offer to settle made before the commencement of proceedings may be taken into account when making any order as to costs. An important point to note is that, if the claimant in a mixed money and non-money claim accepts the Part 36 payment, he will also be treated as accepting the Part 36 offer. If the claimant accepts, he or she will be entitled to his costs. Providing the payment in is made at least 21 days before the trial and if the claimant rejects it and fails to recover more at the trial, the claimant will have to pay the defendant's costs incurred after the payment in, although the claimant's own costs up to that point can be recovered.

Where the defendant accepts the claimant's Part 36 offer the claimant is entitled to the costs of the proceedings up to the date when the defendant serves notice of acceptance.

Where the claimant does better than his proposed Part 36 offer the court may order interest on the whole or part of the sum at a rate not higher than 10% above base rate. The court may also order that the claimant is entitled to costs on an indemnity basis from the date the defendant could have accepted the offer without needing the court's permission and award interest on those costs at a rate not exceeding 10% above base rate.

A carefully calculated Part 36 payment in is therefore an important tactical defence weapon since the costs risk puts great pressure on the claimant to settle for rather less than might be received at a trial. The best defence tactic is probably to make the payment in early in the action, to maximise the risk of later costs, and to make one, or at the most two payments (to make more smacks of weakness). The payment must be sufficiently large as to put real doubt into the mind of the claimant's advisers that it is likely to be beaten at the trial, while offering a real saving to the defendant.

Further, the post-payment in costs awarded to the defendant if the payment in is not beaten at the trial will be set off against the damages payable by the defendant.

Because of these risks, the claimant's solicitors must advise the client carefully both orally and in writing and, in a substantial case, obtain counsel's advice.

6.1.3 Procedure: formal requirements of Part 36

When making the payment in, the procedure is as follows:

1   Form N242A must be used to accompany the payment into court.

2   It can relate to the whole claim or any part of it or to any issue that arises in it.

3   It must state whether it relates to the whole claim or any part of it or to an issue that arises in it and if so to which part or issue.

3   A Part 36 offer may be made by reference to an interim payment.

4   A Part 36 offer made not less than 21 days before the trial must:

   (i)   be expressed to remain open for acceptance for 21 days from the date it is made; and

   (ii) provide that, after the 21 days, the offeree may only accept if the parties agree liability for costs or the court gives permission.

5   Similar provisions apply if the offer is made less than 21 days before trial save that there is no requirement that it remains open for 21 days.

6   If a Part 36 offer is withdrawn it will not have the consequences set out in Part 36.

It is of critical importance that the defendant lets the claimant know how much the latter will receive and how much is retained for the purposes of recoupment. The form helps in making it clear what sum is actually being paid into court and what sum is retained for recoupment purposes.

Offers made before proceedings are issued

If a party makes an offer to settle before proceedings begin which complies with Part 36, then the court will take into account that offer when assessing costs.

The offer must:

(a) be expressed to remain open for at least 21 days after the date on which it was made;

(b) if made by a potential defendant to the action, include an offer to pay the costs of the offeree up to the date 21 days after it was made; and

(c) otherwise comply with the requirements of Part 36.

If proceedings are subsequently issued, the defendant who has made such an offer must subsequently make a Part 36 payment within 14 days of service of the claim form. The amount of the payment must be no less than the sum offered before proceedings commenced.

A claimant who is faced with an offer and a subsequent payment may not, after the proceedings have begun, accept an offer under para 36(2) or the subsequent Part 36 payment without the permission of the court. In such cases, the claimant will have to justify late acceptance and often be required to pay the costs of issue and the defendant's costs since issue.

How the payment in is made

The defendant must file the Part 36 payment notice and copy for service if required and send a cheque or draft payable to HMPG.

The court will serve the notice unless the offeror informs the court, when making the payment in, that he has served it. A certificate of service is required if the offeror serves it.

Variation of Part 36 payment may not be made without the court's permission.

A Part 36 offer or any variation is only effective when received by the offeree. Acceptance of a Part 36 payment is effective when notice of the acceptance is received by the offeror.

6.1.4 Split trials

The defendant or the claimant may make a written offer to any other party to accept liability up to a specified proportion.

This could have the same effect as a payment into court if the defendant is held to be no more to blame than the proportion offered. This is therefore a good means for a defendant to redress the extra pressure he or she may be put under if a split trial is ordered; it may also be a way of forcing a co-defendant to join in a settlement.

6.2   Part 20 proceedings – joining new parties in an action

Part 20 of the CPR deals with:

(a) a counterclaim by a defendant against the claimant or against the claimant and some other person;

(b) a claim by a defendant against any person (whether or not they are already a party) for contribution, indemnity or some other remedy.

If the defendant wishes to counterclaim against a person other than the claimant, then the defendant must apply to the court for an order that that person be joined as a defendant to the counterclaim. This application can be made without notice and, when making the order, the court will make case management directions. A defendant who has filed an acknowledgement of service or a defence can make a Part 20 claim for contribution or indemnity against another defendant by filing a notice containing a statement of the nature of the grounds of his claim and serving notice on the other defendant.

6.2.1 Other Part 20 claims

If the Part 20 claim is not a counterclaim or a claim for contribution or indemnity from a co-defendant then:

(a) the Part 20 claim is made when the court issues a Part 20 claim form;

(b) the defendant can make a Part 20 claim without the court's permission if the Part 20 claim is issued before or at the same time as he files the defence;

(c) the defendant can make a Part 20 claim at any other time, but needs the court's permission. An application for permission to make a Part 20 claim can be made without notice unless the court directs otherwise;

(d) particulars of the Part 20 claim must be contained in or served with a Part 20 claim.

6.2.2 Title of proceedings where there are Part 20 claims

The title of every Part 20 claim must include:

(a) the full name of each party;

(b) his status in the proceedings.

Where there is more than one Part 20 claim, the parties to the first Part 20 claim should be described as 'Part 20 claimant (1st claim)' and 'Part 20 defendant (1st claim)': the parties to the second Part 20 claim should be described as 'Part 20 claimant (2nd claim)' and 'Part 20 defendant (2nd claim)'; and so on.

6.2.3 Procedure for serving a Part 20 claim form on a non-party

When serving a Part 20 claim on a person who is not already a party, it must be accompanied by:

(a) a form for defending the claim;

(b) a form for admitting the claim;

(c) a form for acknowledgement of service; and

(d) a copy of every statement of case which has already been served in the proceedings and such other documents as the court may direct.

6.2.4 Part 20 hearing

It should not be taken for granted that the Part 20 claim will automatically be heard with the first claim. The court has the power to order that matters be dealt with separately and to decide the order in which matters are tried. This will be considered at any case management conference and the court must have regard to:

(a) the connection between the Part 20 claim and the claim made by the claimant against the defendant;

(b) whether the Part 20 claimant is seeking substantially the same remedy which some other party is claiming from him; and

(c) whether the Part 20 claimant wants the court to decide any question connected with the subject matter of proceedings –

   (i) not only between existing parties but also between existing parties and a person not already an existing party; or

   (ii) against an existing party not only in capacity or in a capacity in which he is already a party but also in some further capacity.

6.2.5 Judgment in default on Part 20 claims

Special rules apply where the Part 20 claim is not a counterclaim or a claim by a defendant for an indemnity or contribution against another defendant. If the party against whom the Part 20 claim is made fails to file an acknowledgement of service or a defence in respect of the Part 20 claim, he is deemed to admit the Part 20 claim and is bound by any decision or judgment in the main proceedings in so far as it is relevant to any matter arising in the Part 20 claim. Further, if default judgment is given against the Part 20 claimant, it is possible to obtain default judgment on a Part 20 claim. The Part 20 claimant can obtain judgment by filing a request. However, the Part 20 claimant cannot enter judgment without the court's permission if:

(a) he has not satisfied the default judgment which has been given against him;

(b) he wishes to obtain judgment for any remedy other than a contribution or indemnity.

However, an application for the court's permission can be made without notice unless the court otherwise directs.

6.3   Interim payments

6.3.1 Purpose of interim payments

These payments are payments on account of any damages which the defendant may be ordered to pay. They are designed to meet the complaint that claimants with strong cases often have to wait long periods before receiving any compensation, for example, because the claimant's medical position has not yet stabilised. Claimants' solicitors should consider applying for these, since they can greatly reduce any financial hardship the claimant may be suffering (though they are not limited to such cases). They may also be a means of financing the case (see Chapter 3).

6.3.2 Procedural points

The important procedural points are that:

(a) the claimant cannot apply for an order for an interim payment before the end of the period for filing an acknowledgement of service by the defendant against whom the application is made;

(b) the claimant can make more than one application for an order for an interim payment;

(c) a copy of the application notice for an order for an interim payment must be served at least 14 days before the hearing of the application and it must be supported by evidence.

(d) If the respondent to the application wishes to rely on written evidence, this must be filed and served on every other party to the application at least seven days before the application. The applicant must then file evidence in reply at least three days before the hearing.

6.3.3 Evidence in support

An application for an interim payment must be supported by evidence dealing with:

(a) the sum of money sought by way of an interim payment;

(b) the items or matters in respect of which the interim payment is sought;

(c) the sum of money for which final judgment is likely to be given;

(d) the reasons for believing that the requisites for obtaining an interim payment are set out;

(e) any other relevant matters;

(f) details of special damages and past and future loss;

(g) in a claim under the Fatal Accidents Act 1976 details of the person on whose behalf the claim is made and the nature of the claim.

Any documents in support of the application should be exhibited including the medical reports.

6.3.4 Conditions to be satisfied

The court can make an order for interim payment if:

(a) the defendant against whom the order is sought has admitted liability to pay damages or some other sum of money to the claimant;

(b) the claimant has obtained judgment against the defendant for damages to be assessed;

(c) the court is satisfied that, if the claim went to trial, the claimant would obtain judgment for a substantial amount of money against the defendant from whom he or she is seeking an order for an interim payment and the defendant is insured in respect of the claim or the defendant is a public body.

6.3.5 The compensation recovery position

If the application is not a consent application and the defendant is liable to pay recoverable benefits, the defendant must obtain a certificate of recoverable benefits and a copy of the certificate should be filed at the hearing. The payment made to the claimant will be the net amount, however, for the purposes of the final judgment, the figure will be the gross amount.

6.3.6 Multi-defendants

The court can make any order for interim payment of damages against any defendant if:

(a) it is satisfied that if the claim went to trial that the claimant would obtain judgment for substantial damages against at least one of the defendants;

(b) each of the defendants are insured, covered by a Motor Insurers Bureau agreement or a public body.

6.3.7 The amount of the interim payment

Part 25.7(4) states that the court must not order an interim payment of more than a reasonable proportion of the likely amount of final judgment. The court must take into account both contributory negligence and any relevant set-off or counterclaim.

6.4 Common problems and their solutions

Problem	Solution
Defendant makes payment into court.	Claimant's solicitor reviews liability, quantum and evidence, obtains counsel's opinion on payment if case substantial, and advises client orally and in writing.
Payment into court does include interest.	Although defendant not bound to include interest, if none included the claimant can threaten/continue action to recover the interest.
Can the payment in be passed on to the client if accepted?	Yes, except where the claimant is a minor or a mental patient (payment needs court's consent and money stays in court).

Defendant issues Part 20 notice.	Claimant should consider joining Part 20 defendant into action as an additional defendant. Check whether there is a cause of action against the Part 20 defendant and whether it is appropriate for the claimant to pursue this party.
Claimant seeks large interim payment.	Defendant should review liability (particularly contributory negligence) and quantum and oppose application; or offer payment covering special damages to date less deduction for contributory negligence; and/or make payment into court.

Key points

1 The defendant must normally make a Part 36 payment into court. The claimant can make a Part 36 offer to settle.

2 New parties can be joined into an action by way of Part 20 proceedings.

3 The claimant can apply for an interim payment after the time for filing an acknowledgment of service. The claimant must provide evidence in support and satisfy the court that the claimant will obtain damages against the defendant.

4 An interim payment is subject to compensation recovery. The defendant must pay off the Compensation Recovery Unit figure before making any payment to the claimant.

7 Case Management, Disclosure and Inspection

This chapter looks at disclosure and inspection of documents under the Civil Procedure Rules (CPR) and issues relating to case management.

The period after the defence is filed is an important one. A party who understands principles of case management and can use these effectively can achieve a significant advantage over the less active party. At this stage the parties have a duty to the court to assist in case management. However, to assist their clients, both sides should try to keep the momentum up, with the aim of securing a favourable settlement.

Case management is dealt with first. The directions made enable the court to identify and crystallise the issues and make any orders that may be needed. We will then consider the important topic of discovery, that is, disclosure of documents.

For more detail see O'Hare and Hill, *Civil Litigation* (2001); Pritchard *et al*, *Personal Injury Litigation* (2002); and Style and Hollander's *Documentary Evidence* (2000).

7.1 Case management

7.1.1 The tracks

The court is under a duty to manage cases. In the first instance, this involves allocating a case to a track.

(a) The small claims track normally involves cases with a value of less than £5,000. However, in personal injury cases the small claims track is only relevant where damages for the pain, suffering and loss of amenity is less than £1,000. There is a requirement therefore to state, in the claim form and in the particulars of claim, whether or not the claim for pain and suffering exceeds £1,000.

(b) The fast track involves cases where damages are less than £15,000 and the trial will take less than one day. If, for some reason, the trial will take more than one day, it is not suitable for allocation to the fast track.

(c) The multitrack involves cases of more than £15,000 or that are otherwise unsuitable for allocation to the fast track.

7.1.2 The allocation questionnaire

The first important document in a case is the allocation questionnaire. This must be filled in with some care and returned within the period specified in the questionnaire.

7.1.3 Applications in the course of proceedings

Many practitioners will avoid making applications in straightforward cases and seek to get the matter to trial. However, if an application is necessary the solicitor should:

(a) consider whether an application is, in fact, necessary. An application can be made in writing, alternatively it may be prudent to wait and seek directions at the next case management conference;

(b) consider whether the costs of the application can be justified (remember that an order for costs may be made against you);

(c) ensure that the application has a realistic time estimate.

Making the application

The application is made on Form N244. The applicant must serve a copy of the notice on each respondent to the application together with any evidence relied upon and a draft order should also be prepared and served. The applicant is required to state what the order is seeking and why the applicant is seeking the order. The evidence can be printed on the form and relied upon so long as it is supported by a statement of truth. The application must be served as soon as practicable after it was filed.

Prior to the hearing, each party should serve a schedule of costs so that the court can assess costs at the end of the hearing.

When attending the application it is important that an order for costs is made. If there is no order for costs at all then neither party can recover costs for attending.

Telephone hearings

Less controversial applications, and consent applications, can be made without a hearing. In some circumstances, the court can direct that the hearing takes place by telephone. The applicant's legal representative must arrange the conference. The call is recorded by British Telecom and a tape sent to the court.

Disclosure and inspection

Disclosure is the process by one part to the other of the existence of documents that are relevant to the issues in the case and which are not privileged. This process – which should in theory take place at the pre-action protocol stage – is one that should enable the parties to test the strength of their cases and so perhaps encourage settlement.

Accordingly, this is an important topic, but is one that is often taken insufficiently seriously in personal injury claims because solicitors often feel it is unlikely that there will be any relevant documents.

Remember also that it is the solicitors' duty to obtain from the client and preserve any relevant documents, however embarrassing they may be to the client's case. The solicitor cannot be a party to such documents disappearing or not being disclosed (unless they are privileged). Disclosed documents may only be used for the purpose of the current proceedings, unless they have been read out in open court, or unless the party obtaining discovery applies to be released from this application.

Documents to look out for

(a) The accident book kept by employer – look for entries regarding the current and previous similar accidents.

(b) Employer's complaints book.

(c) Minutes of any safety committee.

(d) Statements made to the employer or hospital after the accident if not made mainly with regard to future litigation.

(e) Maintenance records of machine or vehicles involved in the accident.

(f) Employee's sick notes.

(g) Claimant's special damage documents.

Standard disclosure

Part 31 of the CPR deals with disclosure of documents and applies to both the fast and multitracks. In most cases, all that is necessary is standard disclosure.

Part 31.2 defines disclosure:

> A party discloses a document by stating that the document exists or has existed.

Part 31.4 defines document:
In this Part–

> 'document' means anything in which information of any description is recorded; and
>
> 'copy', in relation to a document, means anything onto which information recorded in the document has been copied, by whatever means and whether directly or indirectly.

7.1.4 Standard disclosure is the norm

Part 31.5 makes it clear that, when a court makes an order to give disclosure, it is an order to give standard disclosure unless the court orders otherwise. Further, the court can dispense with or limit standard disclosure and the parties may agree in writing to dispense with or to limit standard disclosure.

Standard disclosure defined

Part 31.6 defines standard disclosure:

> Standard disclosure requires a party to disclose only –
> (a) the documents on which he relies; and
> (b) the documents which –
>   (i)   adversely affect his own case;
>   (ii) adversely affect another party's case; or
>   (iii) support another party's case; and
> (c) the documents which he is required to disclose by a relevant practice direction.

7.1.5 The duty of search

The fact that standard disclosure takes place does not, however, mean that the litigator can afford to relax and that obligations on disclosure cannot be ignored. Part 31.7 imposes a duty on a party giving standard disclosure to make a reasonable search for documents failing with Pt 31.6. The factors relevant in deciding the reasonableness of a search include:

(a) the number of documents involved;

(b) the nature and complexity of the proceedings;

(c) the ease and expense of retrieval of any particular document; and

(d) the significance of any documents which is likely to be located during the search.

Where a party has not searched for a category or class of document on the grounds that to do so would be unreasonable, he must state this in the disclosure statement and identify the category or class of document.

7.1.6 Duty of disclosure limited to documents which are or have been in a party's control

A party's duty to disclose documents is limited to documents which are or have been in his control. This is defined as:

(a) a document which is or was in his physical possession; or

(b) a document which the party has or has had a right to possession of; or

(c) a document which the party has or has had a right to inspect or take copies of.

7.1.7 Disclosure of copies

A party need not disclose more than one copy of a document. However, a copy of a document that contains a modification, obliteration or other marking feature, on which a party intends to rely or which adversely affects his case or another party's case or supports another party's case, is treated as a separate document.

7.2 Procedure for standard disclosure

Disclosure is by list, the Practice Direction makes it clear that the list to be used is Form N625. The list must identify the documents in a convenient order and manner and as concisely as possible. It will normally be necessary to list the documents in date order, number them consecutively and to give a concise description. Where a large number of documents fall into a particular category, they may be listed as a category rather than individually. The list must indicate those documents in respect of which the party claims a right or duty to withhold inspection; and those documents which are no longer in the party's control; and say what has happened to those documents.

7.2.1 The disclosure statement

The list must include a disclosure statement. This is a statement made by the party disclosing the documents:

(a) setting out the extent of the search that has been made to locate documents of which disclosure is required;

(b) certifying that he or she understands the duty to disclose documents;

(c) certifying that to the best of his/her knowledge, s/he has carried out that duty.

Where the party making the disclosure statement is a company, firm, association or other organisation, the statement must also:

(a) identify the person making the statement; and

(b) explain why s/he is considered the appropriate person to make the statement.

7.2.2 Additional obligations

The Practice Direction states that the disclosure statement should:

(a) expressly state that the disclosing party believes the extent of the search to have been reasonable in all the circumstances;

(b) in setting out the extent of the search, draw attention to any particular limitations on the extent of the search that were adopted for proportionality reasons and give the reasons why the limitations were not adopted.

7.2.3 Agreement between the parties

The rules make it clear that the parties may agree in writing to disclose documents without making a list and to disclose documents without the disclosing party making a disclosure statement.

7.2.4 Disclosure is a continuing obligation

Where the disclosing party is legally represented, that representative is under a duty to make sure that the person making the disclosing statement understands the duty of disclosure. The obligations continue until the proceedings end. If further documents come to the attention of the disclosing party, they must immediately notify every other party and prepare and serve a supplemental list.

7.3   Specific disclosure or inspection

Part 31.12 allows the court to make an order for specific disclosure or specific inspection. The Practice Direction makes it clear that a party can apply for specific disclosure if he believes that disclosure given by the opposing party is inadequate. The application notice must specify the order that the applicant intends to ask the court to make and must be supported by evidence. The grounds on which the order is sought may be set out in the application itself but, if not, then it must be set out in the evidence in support. The court will take into account all the circumstances of the case and, in particular, the overriding objective in Pt 1. The court may order the party to disclose documents specified in the order, the court may also order specific inspection of a document where the other party has stated in their disclosure statement that they will not permit inspection on the grounds that it would be disproportionate to do so.

7.4   The inspection and copying of documents

Part 31.3 gives a party a right of inspection of a disclosed document except where –

(a) the document is no longer in the control of the party who disclosed it; or

(b) the party disclosing the document has a right or a duty to withhold inspection of it; or

(c) a party considers it would be disproportional to the issues in the case to permit inspection of documents within a category and states, in his disclosure statement, that inspection of those documents will not be permitted on the grounds that to do so would be disproportionate.

Part 31.15 states that, where a party has a right to inspect a document, that party wishing to inspect must give written notice of his wish to inspect and the party who disclosed the document must permit inspection not more than seven days after the date on which he received the notice.

Part 31.15(c) states that a party seeking inspection may request a copy of the document, and if he also undertakes to pay reasonable copying costs, the party who disclosed the document must supply him with a copy not more than seven days after the date on which he received the request.

7.5   Inadvertent disclosure of privileged documents

These can only be used with the permission of the court (r 31.20). There is a three stage test:

1   was it evident to the solicitor receiving privileged documents that a mistake had been made? If it was the solicitor should return the documents;

2   if it was not obvious, would it have been obvious to the reasonable solicitor that disclosure of these documents was a mistake? If so, the privilege is retained. Where the case is close to the line, the solicitor should seek to ascertain whether an error has occurred;

3   if it would not have been obvious to the reasonable solicitor, privilege is lost.

7.5.1   Failure to disclose documents or permit inspection

Part 31.21 states that a party may not rely on any document which he fails to disclose or in respect of which he fails to permit inspection unless the court gives permission.

7.5.2   Subsequent use of disclosed documents

Part 31.22 reiterates the old law when it states that a party to whom a document has been disclosed can only use it for the purpose of the proceedings in which it is disclosed, except where:

(a) the document has been read to or by the court, or referred to, at a hearing which has been held in public;

(b) the court gives permission;

(c) the party who disclosed the document and the person to whom the document belongs agree.

The court has power to make an order restricting or prohibiting the use of a document which has been disclosed, even when it is read out in court or referred to at a hearing which has been held in public.

7.6   Disclosure in specific tracks

7.6.1   Fast track

Directions will be given on the allocation of a case to the fast track. These should include provision for the disclosure of documents and will usually be specified as standard disclosure. However, if the court does not consider this to be appropriate it may direct that no disclosure take place or specify the documents to be disclosed. The Practice Direction – the fast track (PD 28) proposes that the timetable for disclosure should generally be four weeks after the notice of allocation.

7.6.2 Multitrack

The court must give directions and/or fix a case management conference when the case is allocated to the multitrack. The directions must include an order as to disclosure and Practice Direction – the multitrack (PD29) states that the court may limit the disclosure to standard or less. The court may also direct that disclosure may take place by supplying copies of all documents, but the parties must either serve a disclosure statement with the copies or agree to disclose without such a statement.

Key points

1 The first important case management decision is which track the matter should be allocated to. The claimant should be aware of which track is appropriate prior to the issue of proceedings.

2 Both parties must complete and return the allocation questionnaire within the appropriate time. Failure to do so can lead to a claim and/or defence being struck out.

3 When making an application use Form N244. Be certain that the application is necessary and justifiable. Ensure that the opportunity is used to deal with all relevant case management issues.

4 Litigators must be aware of the important duties when undertaking disclosure and inspection. In particular, the duty to disclose documents that are adverse to your own case.

8 Preparing for Trial

This chapter considers the final steps needed to assemble the evidence and arrange for the case to be listed for trial and tried. As the trial itself is likely to be handled either by counsel or by a solicitor with some experience, it will not be dealt with here. (In any event, only a tiny proportion of cases go to a hearing: see Chapter 9.) On preparations generally, see O'Hare and Hill, *Civil Litigation* (2001) or Pritchard, *Personal Injury Litigation* (2002).

8.1 Instructing counsel to advise on evidence

It is often useful to have counsel's advice on evidence at an early stage, or at least before the automatic directions in case there is any need to seek different directions. However, in a case that will be argued by counsel, it is highly desirable for counsel to assess the available evidence at the latest once discovery is complete and before the trial is in prospect. This is likely to be particularly important in more complex accident at work cases where there is, perhaps, a conflict of engineering evidence.

On how to instruct counsel, see 4.7. Counsel will particularly need to see the proofs of evidence, documents disclosed on discovery, reports from experts, the police or the Health and Safety Executive, plans and photographs and an updated schedule of special damages. The advice should identify the witnesses to be called and the documents to be used and deal with any other outstanding matters such as hearsay notices, notices to admit etc.

8.2   Documentary evidence

8.2.1 Documents

There may well be documents which the other party is unlikely to dispute if satisfied they are genuine, for example, letters from the DSS and other special damage documentation. However, all documents not contained in witness statements, affidavits, expert opinion, given orally or as hearsay may be admitted provided notice is given. A counter-notice, requiring the maker of the document to attend, may be served. Under Pt 31, a party is deemed to admit to the authenticity of a document disclosed unless he serves a notice that the document must be proved at trial (r 32.19(1) of the CPR).

Remember, also, that it is normally necessary to use original and not copy documents. If the original is in the possession of a non-party, then that person can be served with a witness summons (see 8.3.2). If, however, the original is in the hands of your opponent, then you should serve a notice to produce the original at the trial. However it should be borne in mind that s 8 of the Civil Evidence Act (CEA) 1995 provides that any document admissible as evidence may be proved simply by production of that document or even by production of a copy. The copy must be authenticated as approved by the court, but if this is done it is irrelevant how far removed from the copy the original is.

8.2.2 Experts' reports

Ensure that your expert evidence is no more than a year old at most and, if necessary, obtain an updating report. Ensure that the directions for using such evidence have been obtained where necessary (see Chapter 7) and complied with. You cannot use an expert in the case unless you have the court's permission. Try and agree the reports if possible. It may be helpful for experts to have a meeting before the trial in order to identify the areas in dispute. Often, the court will order this in any event. The experts will be expected to prepare a schedule setting out the issues on which they agree and disagree. On the fast track, the courts will be particularly keen to avoid experts giving evidence, it is important to consider whether this is appropriate. There may be cases in which experts need to be called.

8.2.3 Plans and photographs

These should be exchanged and agreed if possible.

8.2.4 Previous convictions etc

Ask the defendant to admit the fact of the conviction if this has not already been done in the defence. If necessary, a notice to admit the fact can be served (see Chapter 8). As a precaution, obtain the certificate of conviction from the criminal court concerned. Ask the defendant to agree that the coroner's notes of any inquest should be admissible.

8.2.5 Preparing bundles of documents

At least 14 days before the date set for trial, the defendant must notify the claimant of the documents he wants included in the trial bundle. The claimant must lodge the bundle no more than seven or less than three days before the trial date. The bundles must be paginated and indexed.

The bundle must contain:

(a) the claim form and all statements of case;

(b) a case summary and/or chronology as appropriate;

(c) requests for further information and the response to such requests;

(d) all witness statements to be relied on as evidence;

(e) any notices of intention to rely on hearsay evidence;

(f) any medical reports and responses to them;

(g) any experts' reports and responses to them;

(h) any order giving directions as to the conduct of the trial;

(i) any other necessary documents.

The originals of the documents contained in the trial bundle together with copies of any other court orders should be available at court.

It the bundle is more than 100 pages, numbered dividers should be placed at intervals between groups of documents.

8.3   Witnesses

Drafting a witness statement is an important skill. In many cases, this will constitute the only evidence in chief which that witness is allowed to give. For this reason, more detailed guidance as to drafting witness statements can be found in Chapter 12.

8.3.1   Avoiding the attendance of witnesses

Always try to avoid having to call witnesses by attempting to agree the evidence with your opponent. A means of putting pressure on the opponent to do so is to serve a notice to admit facts. The sanction is that, if the party served with the notice fails to admit the facts, they could be liable for the costs of proving those facts regardless of the outcome of the case. If a witness is too ill to travel or likely to die prior to the trial, there is a provision in CPR Pt 34 for a witness to be examined prior to the trial by a judge or an examiner appointed by the court. Such deposition evidence is likely to be regarded as more powerful than evidence given by way of a witness statement. Where it is clear that such evidence would be beneficial, the solicitor should apply to the court specifying the details of the deponent. Where a witness has died or is going abroad for a long time, or cannot reasonably be expected to remember the events in question, then you should, under s 1 of the CEA 1995, be able to rely on hearsay evidence. That is to say, A told B about events that A had personally perceived, B's evidence may be admitted as 'first hand' hearsay.

If you wish to use such hearsay evidence, then you must follow the procedure laid down in s 2 of the CEA 1995. That is to say, serve notice of your intention to rely on such evidence to the court and the other parties to the action. This is implemented by r 33.2 of the CPR. If a party intends to rely on hearsay evidence contained in a witness statement, that statement must be served on the other parties. If no oral evidence is to be given in respect of the statement, the other parties must be informed of this with reasons for the non-attendance. This notice must be served no later than the last date of service of witness statements.

A counter-notice of intent to challenge the hearsay evidence by attacking the credibility of the person who made the original statement, must be served within 14 days of service of the hearsay notice.

When seeking to admit or challenge hearsay evidence, s 4 of the CEA 1995 should be borne in mind. It deals with the weight the court should attach to hearsay evidence. Factors are: the reasonableness of the non-attendance at court of the maker of the original statement, whether the statement was contemporaneous, any motive of a person to conceal or misrepresent and whether circumstances are such that a proper evaluation of the evidence is impossible due to non-attendance.

8.3.2 Witnesses who need to attend

In respect of those witnesses who will need to attend the trial, including the client, it is important to send them (in good time before the case may be heard) an updated proof of evidence for them to check and amend if necessary. As this will be the basis of the advocate's examination in chief of the witness, it should not contain any inadmissible material such as non-expert opinion or hearsay not covered by the CEA 1995. Ask the witness to sign and date the proof in case he should die or become seriously ill before the trial, since the proof would then be admissible.

Also, find out whether the witness is likely to attend the trial voluntarily.

If there is some doubt about this, or in some cases, if it will help the witness (such as some expert witnesses) to break other commitments, serve the witness with a witness summons. This may require the witness to attend to give evidence (subpoena *ad testificandum*) or to produce a document (subpoena *duces tecum*).

To obtain a witness summons, under Pt 34, complete Form N20. The witness may be served either personally or by post, a reasonable time before the trial.

8.3.3 Exchange of witness statements

The exchange of witness statements is mandatory (Pt 32.4). For the procedure for drafting a witness statement, see later in this book.

8.4 Real evidence

Ensure that arrangements are made to bring to court vital objects that the judge may want to see in order to understand what is alleged to have occurred, for example, the defective brake part or the piece of machinery alleged to have caused the injury. If this is not feasible, for example, because of their size, and the position cannot be adequately explained by photographs, then agree with the other side that it will be necessary for the judge to view the object and/or accident scene in person (Ord 21, r 6 of the County Court Rules).

8.5   Other pre-trial points

8.5.1 Compliance with directions for trial

Keep up the pressure on your opponent and apply for the action to be dismissed or defence to be struck out unless the orders are complied with within the time fixed in the automatic directions or ordered by the court.

8.5.2 Possible settlement of the claim

It is still likely that the case will settle, even if only at the door of the court. However, beware the pressure that can be brought to bear on a claimant who has never been through court proceedings before.

8.5.3 Updating the special damages calculation

Once updated figures are prepared, the claimant should try to agree them with the defence. Service of a notice to admit documents or a notice of intention of using hearsay evidence may encourage agreement.

8.5.4 Briefing counsel

Because of the need to be ready for trial as soon as the case is set down, it is advisable to prepare the brief at this stage. You will normally wish to use counsel who has been advising throughout, but the brief should be a full one so that the case can be taken over if necessary by counsel who has not previously been involved.

The brief should enclose the statement of claim, reports, agreed bundles of documents, a schedule of special damages and previous opinions of counsel. It should outline the facts and the issues in dispute, the evidence and any difficulties with it, and any particularly salient or recent developments in the relevant law. For a specimen brief, see O'Hare and Hill, *Civil Litigation*.

If no settlement is forthcoming, it will then be necessary to deliver the brief and to agree the brief fee. This is done over the telephone with counsel's clerk, professional ethics preventing counsel from dealing with the matter.

It may also be helpful for counsel to meet the client in conference at his or her chambers if this has not already occurred. This will convey to counsel the client's likely calibre as a witness, it should give the client added confidence in the person who will be his or her representative at the trial, and, sometimes, it can bring home to the client the difficulties in the case more effectively than advice from the solicitor with whom there is continuing contact.

Preparing a schedule of costs

In a fast track trial, it is necessary for both parties to serve schedules of costs. This is also necessary in multitrack cases where the hearing will be less than one day. The court will then assess costs at the end of the case. It is very important that these schedules are served and lodged at least 24 hours before the hearing.

8.6   The trial

8.6.1   The solicitor's role

This book assumes that the reader will not personally be presenting cases. The reader's role will, thus, be the important one of ensuring the attendance at court of the client and witnesses. In fast track cases, a solicitor will only recover £250 in costs *if* the court considers it reasonable for the solicitor to be there. If the solicitor does not attend, it is important to ensure that the advocate has all potential relevant documents. If the solicitor does attend the trial it will be necessary to liaise between the client and witnesses, on the one hand, and counsel (who cannot discuss the case with the witnesses) on the other. It will also be necessary to take a note of the evidence, particularly when your advocate is on his or her feet.

8.6.2   After the judgment

It is important to remind the advocate to ask the judge to deal with the following matters where appropriate.

Interest on the damages

Costs against the opponent – remember to ask the judge to deal with any interlocutory applications where costs were reserved, and to point out where your client is entitled to costs whatever the outcome (for example, because of service of a notice to admit).

Payment into court

This may substantially affect the entitlement to costs.

8.6.3 Remaining matters

The following points may need attention:

(a) A notice of appeal from a circuit judge must be served not later than 14 days after the date of judgment order and from a district judge within 14 days of the judgment. Permission is required for all relevant appeals from the district judge to the circuit or High Court Judge or to the Court of Appeal.

(b) Detailed guidance on the appeal procedure can be found in the *Manual of Civil Appeals* (di Mambro *et al*).

Assessment of costs

If there is no assessment at the end of the trial the judge will usually order that costs be assessed if not agreed. Try to agree costs, but, if this is not possible, remember that both parties can make Part 36 offers in relation to costs.

8.7   Common problems and their solutions

Defendant delays agreeing special damages documents.	Claimant threatens/serves notice to admit special damage or notice of intention of using such documents as hearsay evidence on grounds that authors cannot reasonably be expected to remember the information in them.
Witness reluctant to attend court.	Remind witness that damages will be paid by insurers. Take signed and dated proof of evidence. Threaten/ serve witness summons. Once in witness box, can be cross-examined on proof if proves hostile.

Claimant's medical condition not stable.	Consider applying for split trial, liability only being dealt with at this stage. But disadvantageous to claimant if case strong on quantum but weak on liability.

Key points

1 Remember the importance of witness statements.

2 Ensure that the trial bundle is properly prepared and contains all the relevant documents.

3 Ensure that the schedule of costs is served in good time.

4 Ensure that all the witnesses know where to attend and are willing to attend or have been summonsed to attend.

9 Early Conclusion of Cases

This chapter will consider the commonest ways in which personal injury actions may terminate without the need for a trial, as indeed is the case in the great majority of actions.

For more detail see O'Hare and Hill, *Civil Litigation* or Pritchard, *Personal Injury Litigation*.

9.1 Settlement before or after proceedings issued

9.1.1 Settlement before proceedings have commenced

Most personal injury cases are settled without the need to start proceedings. The settlement terms are recorded in the correspondence between the solicitors and insurers. The latter may ask the claimant to sign a receipt confirming acceptance of the payment in full and final settlement of the claim. As problems of enforcement of settlements rarely arise in personal injury actions, no other formalities are needed except in the case of minors and other people under a disability such as mental patients, where the court will have to approve the settlement (see 9.2).

However, it is important to explain the effect of a proposed settlement to the client. It will be wise to obtain counsel's opinion on the proposed settlement in substantial cases. Obtain written confirmation from the client that he or she understands and accepts the settlement terms. Finally, ensure that the position as to costs has been agreed.

9.1.2 Settlement after proceedings have commenced

Informing the court

If the case has been allocated a trial date or trial window, the court must be informed of the settlement and the parties should jointly apply to withdraw the action.

Is a court order desirable?

An order has the advantages of certainty, and it will allow for costs to be taxed if they have not been agreed. The usual procedure is to obtain a stay of the proceedings, freezing them either temporarily or, once all the terms of the settlement have been agreed, permanently, except for the possibility of returning to court to ensure the carrying out of any of the terms agreed (a 'Tomlin' order). The order should also refer to any interim payments already made, provide for payment out of any money in court, deal with which party is to receive the interest on money in court, and for costs between the parties and for assessment of any costs where the party is publicly funded.

Obtaining the consent order

The claimant will prepare a notice of application for judgment to be entered in the agreed terms, obtain the defendant's consent and then lodge it at court. The court will send sealed copies to both parties.

Money in court

The court will send the money in court to the claimant's solicitor on the making of the consent order.

9.2 Persons under a disability

When settling claims on behalf of minors and mental patients, the court's approval to the settlement will be needed before the settlement can be accepted if proceedings have started (CPR 21.10 and PD 6). This is also so in fatal cases where a payment into court has to be apportioned between the 1934 and 1976 Act claims and/or between dependants. Application is made by the Pt 8 procedure if proceedings have not already begun. In all but the clearest cases, counsel's opinion on the merits of the settlement should be obtained. It is not wise to accept any suggestion by insurers that payment should be made simply against a receipt signed by the next friend; indeed, the insurers should be prepared to pay the claimant's costs in obtaining the court's approval.

9.2.1 Part 8 procedure (for precedent see Chapter 11)

This is a special procedure for coming before the court when there is
no substantial dispute as to facts. This is meant to be used in cases such
as:

(a) minor approval summonses;

(b) cases where a claim for provisional damages has been settled prior
to issue but a court order is needed.

In these cases, the claimant must set out in the claim form:

(a) details of what the court is being asked to decide;

(b) details of any enactment relied upon;

(c) whether the claimant or defendant are acting in a representative
capacity.

In the High Court, applications for approval of settlement are made to
masters and appointments are made in their own private rooms. The
procedure is paralleled in the county court. If the claim is a simple one
and the evidence is clear, counsel's opinion is not needed (PD 21).
Where there is any uncertainty over the settlement figure or the sum
involved is large or needs apportioning under the Fatal Accidents Act
1976, then counsel's advice should be obtained. At the settlement
hearing, the claimant's solicitor should have the summons , a copy of
CFO Form 320, completed on the first side, a copy of the child's birth
certificate, any pleadings, if liability is disputed evidence relating to
liability, medical reports, schedule of damages and supporting
documentation, consent of the litigation friend and the approval of the
settlement by the litigation friend. The litigation friend should attend.
The test to be satisfied in order for the court to give its approval to the
settlement is whether the settlement is a reasonable one and for the
benefit of the infant or patient, having regard to all the circumstances
of the case.

If the court does not approve the settlement, the application may
be adjourned to give the parties further opportunities to negotiate.
However, if it is approved, the order will direct by and to whom and
in what amounts the money is to be paid and how the money is to be
applied or otherwise dealt with. The next friend can, however, apply
for payment of expenses and for payments for the child's benefit, such
as alterations to the home or a holiday to help recuperation. The
claimant's money will be invested until he is old enough to manage
his own affairs save for the necessary expenditure to maintain the
claimant whilst he is under a disability. If the claimant is a mental patient

the settlement moneys will usually be transferred to the Court of Protection.

In cases where the settlement is approved, the usual order is to direct costs to be assessed on the standard basis.

9.3   Default judgments: summary judgment

9.3.1 Default judgments

Judgment can be obtained if the defendant fails to file an acknowledgment of service or defence within the proper time. Such judgment will be judgment on liability with damages and interest to be assessed later and costs to be assessed.

Note that the leave of the court will be needed if the defendant is under a disability or the claimant is claiming provisional damages.

Such default judgments may be set aside on the application of the defendant, but the defendant will usually have to show a good reason for allowing the judgment to be entered (such as illness) and that there is a possible defence.

9.3.2 Summary judgment (Pt 24)

Either the claimant or defendant may apply for summary judgment. The grounds for summary judgment are that the claimant/defendant has no reasonable grounds of successfully succeeding or defending the claim or issue, and there is no other reason why the case should not be disposed of at trial; see *Swain v Hillman & Gay* [2000] PIQR P51.

The application can be made at the time of issue either after the filing of the acknowledgement of service or a defence. If an application for summary judgment is made after filing of the acknowledgement of service, it will stay the filing of the defence. Summary judgment is ideally sought when the claimant files his allocation questionnaire after service of defence and before the claim is allocated to the relevant track. The application is made on notice; this must include a statement that it is an application for summary judgment and made under Pt 24. The notice must identify concisely any point of law or provision in the document on which the application relies and it must state that the application is made because the applicant believes that on the evidence the respondent has no real prospect of success. The applicant must state that he knows of no reason why the matter should not proceed to trial. Thus, when making the application, the solicitor must be quite clear that she has researched all the avenues of evidence. The respondent must be given 14 days' notice of the date fixed for the hearing and the issues it is proposed that the court will deal with on the application. Furthermore, the respondent must file evidence in reply at least seven days before the hearing. Evidence in reply from the applicant must be filed at least three working days prior to the hearing.

The court may make conditional orders, however, there is a lack of clarity as to what powers the court has in relation to the defendant. If the claimant is successful in obtaining summary judgments on liability provision will need to be made to assess damages. The matter will go to a case management hearing for directions for this purpose.

9.3.3 Judgment on admissions

If the defendant clearly admits both liability and the fact that the claimant has suffered some damage, whether in the pleadings, correspondence or otherwise, the claimant can proceed to obtain judgment (r 14.6(4)). The request found on the bottom of Form N205(b) may be adapted for this purpose if the court does not supply an appropriate 'practice form'. If the defendant admits liability he may do so by filing a notice on Form N9C which provides for admission of liability with application for the court to determine the amount or with an offer to pay a specified sum. This form is designed for the individual defendant and is not appropriate for an insurance company! This will normally be judgment on liability only as above.

9.4   Striking out, dismissal for want of prosecution, discontinuance

9.4.1 Striking out by the court

The court has the power to strike out all or part of a statement of case under r 3.4(1). This can be done if it discloses no reasonable grounds for bringing or defending the claim, that it is an abuse of the court's process or is otherwise likely to obstruct the just disposal of the proceedings or that there has been a failure to comply with a rule, practice direction or court order.

The court may strike out of its own motion, or upon application by any party. If the court has struck the matter out of its own initiative, the order must state that the affected party may apply to have it set aside, varied or stayed. If the court does not specify a time limit in which to apply to set aside, it must be done within seven days after service of the order.

9.4.2 Dismissal for want of prosecution

The courts have power to do this inherently and under several rules. This is a key defence tactic to deal with cases which the claimant accidentally or deliberately has let `go to sleep', although it is not used as much as formerly. Prior to the Civil Procedure Rules (CPR), the defendant could apply for the action to be dismissed for want of prosecution if it could be shown that the claimant's delay was either intentional and contumelious (insolent), for example, deliberate disobedience to a peremptory order of the court; or that it is inordinate, inexcusable and prejudicial to the fair trial of the action. The whole period of the delay must be looked at and the nearer the limitation period is to expiry the quicker the claimant must act. However, if the limitation period has not expired, the action will not usually be dismissed since the claimant could start another action (*Birkett v James* [1978] AC 297).

These principles established under the old law are unlikely to have much relevance to the CPR, with the sanctions they provides at every stage, although there may remain cases of delay where the principles above have relevance. Under the CPR, the court now has wide powers to deal with non-compliance with time limits and it can make orders which, in many cases, will be more appropriate in dealing with the claimant's delay than the draconian measure of striking out (*Biguzzi v Rank Leisure plc* [1999] 1 WLR 1926). The alternatives are listed in para 2.3 of PD Protocols and include orders for costs and orders depriving the claimant of part of the interest on any damages.

9.4.3 Discontinuance (Pt 38)

The claimant may discontinue an action at anytime, however, costs are usually awarded against the discontinuing party. Where a claimant has received an interim payment, he can only discontinue if the defendant who made the payment consents in writing or the court gives its permission. To discontinue the claimant must file with the court and serve notice of the discontinuance on every party. The defendant has the right to have the notice set aside in certain circumstances, but this application must be made within 28 days of service of the notice of discontinuance. Discontinuance takes effect on the date when the notice is served and the defendant will be entitled to his costs to the date of service of notice.

Key points

1   When acting for minors, or persons under a disability, it is important that approval of the court is obtained for any settlement.

2   If the defendant does not file and acknowledgment of service and/or defence the claimant can obtain default judgment.

3   If the claimant can establish that the defendant does not reasonably have grounds for successfully defending the claim, then it may be possible to obtain summary judgment under Pt 24.

4   If a party delays, or breaches a court order, the court can strike out the action or defence.

10 Basic Precedents and Forms

The following documents illustrate a straightforward personal injury action where the claimant is likely to receive considerable damages since the defendant driver has been convicted of careless driving as a result of his part in the accident, but contributory negligence is raised. This does not prevent the claimant seeking an order for an interim award of damages. It should be assumed that the action is settled without the need for a trial. We then look at the basic forms that are likely to be encountered in a personal injury action.

10.1 Document 1: Particulars of claim

Proceedings are started when the court issues a claim form at the request of the claimant – Form N1. The particulars of claim must be contained in or served with the claim form or be served on the defendant within 14 days after service of the claim form subject to Civil Procedure Rule (CPR) 7.4(2) which lays down that particulars of claim must be served on the defendant no later than the latest time for serving a claim form.

IN THE LUDDENDEN COUNTY COURT   CASE NO: 1999-1234

BETWEEN

SIMON PAINLESS   Claimant

and

MARCUS CONWOW   Defendant

PARTICULARS OF CLAIM

1   On 1 December 1999 at about 8.00 am the Claimant was driving his motor cycle registration number SP 1 along the High Street Luddenden in a northerly direction and had stopped at the junction with Cow Lane.

2   The Claimant was intending to turn right into Cow Lane and was stationary with his right hand indicator flashing.

3   A Ford Cortina motor car registration number RAM 1 owned and driven by the Defendant was proceeding along Cow Lane in an easterly direction.

4   The Defendant's car turned right into the High Street and collided with the Claimant's motor cycle.

5   The collision was caused by the negligence of the Defendant.

PARTICULARS

The defendant was negligent in that he:

*   failed to indicate that he intended to turn right;

*   cut the corner;

*   drove onto the wrong side of the road;

*   failed to apply his brakes and steering in time or at all so as to steer or control his motor car so as to avoid driving into the Claimant;

*   failed to keep any proper look out and/or to observe the presence of the Claimant;

*   drove into collision with the Claimant's vehicle.

6   The Claimant will rely on the fact that on 1 March 2000 the Defendant was convicted at Luddenden Magistrates' Court of careless driving. The conviction is relevant in that it arose out of the happening of the said accident. A plea of guilty was entered, where –upon the Defendant was fined £100 and incurred four penalty points.

7   By reason of the Defendant's negligence the Claimant, who was born on 1 April 1978 has suffered pain, injury, loss and damage.

PARTICULARS OF INJURY

[Note: a medical report should also be served with the Particulars of Claim]

Colles fracture of right wrist

Compound fracture of left femur

Bruising and grazing to the left elbow and thigh

The Claimant has been unable to resume his hobby of shark fishing.

PARTICULARS OF SPECIAL DAMAGE

[Note: a schedule of special damages should also accompany the Particulars of Claim]

Loss of earnings from 1 December 1999 (particularised in schedule served herewith)	£2,800
Value of motor cycle damaged beyond repair	£750
Value of clothing damaged beyond repair (particularised in schedule)	£325
Travelling expenses to and from hospital	£108
Prescriptions	£42
	£4,025

8   Further, pursuant to s 69 of the County Courts Act 1984 the Claimant is entitled to and claims to recover interest on the amount found to be due at such rate and for such period as the Court thinks fit.

STATEMENT OF TRUTH

*(I believe)(The Claimant believes) that the facts stated in these particulars of claim are true.

*I am duly authorised by the Claimant to sign this statement

Full name Joe Bloggs

Name of claimant's solicitor's firm Hugo Fable & Co

signed   position or office held partner *(Claimant)(Litigation friend)(Claimant's solicitor)

*delete as appropriate

Hugo Fable & Co
Tenure Building
University Street
Luddenden

Solicitor for the Claimant

10.2 Document 2: Defence

When served with a claim form there are three forms served with it :

(a) a form for defending the claim (Form N9B);

(b) a form for admitting the claim (Form N9A);

(c) a form for acknowledgement of service (Form N210).

The defendant may choose his method of reply from these three options, however, a failure to reply may result in judgment being entered against him. The precedent set out below is a defence using form N9B.

IN THE LUDDENDEN COUNTY COURT   **CASE NO: 1999-1234**

BETWEEN

SIMON PAINLESS   Claimant

and

MARCUS CONWOW   Defendant

DEFENCE

1   The Defendant admits that on the date and at the place mentioned in the Particulars of Claim a collision occurred between a motor cycle driven by the Claimant and a motor car driven by the Defendant. In all other particulars paragraphs 1, 2, 3 and 4 are denied.

2   The Defendant denies that he was thereby guilty of the alleged or any negligence or that the said negligence was caused as alleged in paragraph 5 of the Particulars of Claim.

3   The Defendant admits the conviction of careless driving as alleged in paragraph 6 of the Particulars of Claim. It is denied that the conviction is relevant to the issues herein.

4   Alternatively the said collision was caused solely, or alternatively contributed to, by the negligence of the Claimant.

PARTICULARS OF NEGLIGENCE

The Claimant was negligent in that he:

* drove too fast;
* failed to keep a proper look out;
* failed to indicate his intention of turning right into Cow Lane;
* continued to turn into Cow Lane when he saw or should have seen the Defendant's car about to turn into his path;
* drove in front of the Defendant's said motor car;
* failed to slow down, stop,swerve or take such other action as was necessary to avoid the said collision.

5   No admissions are made as to the alleged or any pain, injury,loss or damage or as to any entitlement to interest.

STATEMENT OF TRUTH

★(I believe)(The Defendant believes) that the facts stated in this form are true.

★I am duly authorised by the Defendant to sign this statement

Full name

Name of defendant's solicitor's firm Gradgrind & Co

signed   position or office held   ★(Claimant)(Litigation Friend)(Claimant's solicitor)

★delete as appropriate

Gradgrind & Co
14 Jowler Street
Luddenden

Solicitor for the Defendant

10.3 Document 3: Statement in support of interim payment application

Claimant;

S Painless;

First;

28 May 2000

IN THE LUDDENDEN COUNTY COURT   **CASE NO: 1999-1234**

BETWEEN

SIMON PAINLESS   Claimant

and

MARCUS CONWOW   Defendant

FIRST STATEMENT OF SIMON PAINLESS

I SIMON PAINLESS of 14 Goit Side, Luddenden, West Yorkshire state as follows:-

1   I am the Claimant in this action and I make this statement in support of my application for an interim payment.

2   I am advised by my solicitors and I believe that if this action proceeds to trial I will obtain judgment for substantial damages against the Defendant.

3   I refer to the pleadings in this action. As stated in the Particulars of Claim, when the accident occurred I was driving my motor cycle when it was involved in a collision with a car belonging to and owned by the Defendant. The Defendant has admitted that the collision occurred but denied liability.

4   With regards to liability I exhibit hereto and marked 'SP1' a true copy of the Certificate of Conviction which shows that as a result of his driving at the time of the accident the Defendant was convicted of careless driving at the Luddenden Magistrates' Court on 1 March 2000.

5   As a result of the accident I have sustained extensive personal
     injuries, in particular serious injury to my left arm and shoulder.
     It is probable that I will have a permanent disability. There is
     now produced to me and marked 'SP2' a medical report by Mr
     Doyle dated 1 February 2000 confirming the extent of my
     injuries.

6   I have suffered the following special damages at the date of this
     affidavit:

Loss of earnings from 1 December 1999 to 28 May 2000 at the net rate of £600 per month (and continuing)	£4,200
Written off value of motor cycle	£750
Value of clothing damaged beyond repair	£100
Travelling expenses to and from the hospital at £3 per visit (and continuing)	£132
Prescriptions	£50

7   There is now produced to me and exhibited hereto a bundle of
     documents marked 'SP3' containing evidence confirming the
     calculation of special damages.

8   I would ask the Court to accept that if this action proceeds to
     trial I will recover substantial damages from the Defendant and
     grant me an interim payment of £2,500.

I believe that the contents of this statement are true.

10.4 Document 4: Particulars of claim for Pt 8 application seeking approval of the court for offer of settlement to child/person under a disability

IN THE SUTTON ON THE FOREST COUNTY COURT

CASE NO.

JONATHAN GORDON

(A MINOR)   Claimant
by litigation friend

and

THOMAS EDWARD   Defendant

PARTICULARS OF CLAIM

1   The Claimant's claim is for approval of an offer of settlement made by the Defendant arising out of an accident that occurred on 24 May 1998.

2   The Claimant was born on 20 July 1990 and is aged 10.

3   This is an action to which Part 8 of the Civil Procedure Rules applies.

THE FACTS OF THE ACCIDENT

4   On 24 May 1998 the Claimant was a passenger in a motor car driven by the Defendant. The Defendant drove the car into the rear of a vehicle in front of the Defendant's car. As a result of the collision the Claimant suffered injury.

5   The Defendant has admitted liability for the accident. There is no issue between the parties as to liability, the Defendant does not allege contributory negligence.

THE QUESTION WHICH THE CLAIMANT WANTS THE COURT TO DECIDE

6   The question which the Claimant wants the court to decide is whether the offer of settlement made by the Defendant is fair and reasonable and whether the court will give approval to the offer.

7   The offer of settlement that the court is asked to approve is that:

(1)   The Defendant pay the Claimant the sum of £2,000 in full and final settlement of his claim for personal injuries.

(2)   The Defendant do pay the Claimant's costs of this action to be subject to a detailed assessment if not agreed.

WRITTEN EVIDENCE IN SUPPORT

8   The written evidence upon which the Claimant wishes to rely is served herewith:

(1)   The Claimant's statement dated 25 August 2000

(2)   The report of Ms Elizabeth Rosemary Orthopaedic Surgeon dated 26 February 1999 a supplementary report dated 31 March 1999 and an un-dated letter received in June 2000.

AND the Claimant seeks:

(1)   Approval of the offer of settlement made by the Defendant.

(2)   An order that the court give directions for investment of the money until the Claimant reaches the age of 18.

Dated this   day of 2000

By: Benjamin James & Co, Hare Lane, Sutton-on-the-Forest.

Solicitors for the Claimant.

Forms

The following are the forms that you are likely to come across in a personal injury action.

10.6 Claim form (N1)

	In the
Claim Form	
	Claim No.

Claimant

SEAL

Defendant(s)

Brief details of claim

Value

		£
Defendant's name and address	Amount claimed	
	Court fee	
	Solicitor's costs	
	Total amount	
	Issue date	

The court office at

is open between 10 am and 4 pm Monday to Friday. When corresponding with the court, please address forms or letters to the Court Manager and quote the claim number.

N1 Claim form (CPR Part 7) (10.00)   *Printed on behalf of The Court Service*

	Claim No.	

Does, or will, your claim include any issues under the Human Rights Act 1998?   ☐ Yes   ☐ No

Particulars of Claim (attached)(to follow)

Statement of Truth
*(I believe)(The Claimant believes) that the facts stated in these particulars of claim are true.
* I am duly authorised by the claimant to sign this statement

Full name _____

Name of claimant's solicitor's firm _____

signed _____ position or office held _____
*(Claimant)(Litigation friend)(Claimant's solicitor)   (if signing on behalf of firm or company)
*delete as appropriate

Claimant's or claimant's solicitor's address to
which documents or payments should be sent if
different from overleaf including (if appropriate)
details of DX, fax or e-mail.

10.7 Response pack (N9)

Response Pack

You should read the 'notes for defendant' attached to the claim form which will tell you when and where to send the forms

Included in this pack are:

- either Admission Form N9A (if the claim is for a specified amount) or Admission Form N9C (if the claim is for an unspecified amount or is not a claim for money)
- either Defence and Counterclaim Form N9B (if the claim is for a specified amount) or Defence and Counterclaim Form N9D (if the claim is for an unspecified amount or is not a claim for money)
- Acknowledgment of service (see below)

Complete

If you admit the claim or the amount claimed and/or you want time to pay ▶	the admission form
If you admit part of the claim ▶	the admission form and the defence form
If you dispute the whole claim or wish to make a claim (a counterclaim) against the claimant ▶	the defence form
If you need 28 days (rather than 14) from the date of service to prepare your defence, or wish to contest the court's jurisdiction ▶	the acknowledgment of service
If you do nothing, judgment may be entered against you.	

Acknowledgment of Service

Defendant's full name if different from the name given on the claim form

In the	
Claim No.	
Claimant (including ref)	
Defendant	

Address to which documents about this claim should be sent (including reference if appropriate)

	if applicable	
	fax no.	
	DX no.	
Tel. no. Postcode	e-mail	

Tick the appropriate box

1. I intend to defend all of this claim ☐
2. I intend to defend part of this claim ☐
3. I intend to contest jurisdiction ☐

If you file an acknowledgment of service but do not file a defence within 28 days of the date of service of the claim form, or particulars of claim if served separately, judgment may be entered against you.

If you do not file an application within 28 days of the date of service of the claim form, or particulars of claim if served separately, it will be assumed that you accept the court's jurisdiction and judgment may be entered against you.

Signed _____ (Defendant)(Defendant's solicitor) (Litigation friend)

Position or office held (if signing on behalf of firm or company)

Date _____

The court office at

is open between 10 am and 4 pm Monday to Friday. When corresponding with the court, please address forms or letters to the Court Manager and quote the claim number.

N9 -w3- Response Pack (4.99)   Produced on behalf of The Court Service

10.8   Notice of funding of case or claim (N251)

Notice of Funding of Case or Claim

Notice of funding by means of a conditional fee agreement, insurance policy or undertaking given by a prescribed body should be given to the court and all other parties to the case:

* on commencement of proceedings
* on filing an acknowledgment of service, defence or other first document; and
* at any later time that such an arrangement is entered into, changed or terminated

In the	
Claim No.	
Claimant (include Ref)	
Defendant (include Ref)	

Take notice that in respect of [all claims herein] [the following claims . . . .] the case of . . . . (specify name of party)

[is now] [was] being funded by:
(Please tick those boxes which apply)

☐ a conditional fee agreement dated . . . . which provides for a success fee;

☐ an insurance policy issued on (date) . . . . . . by (name of insurers) . . . . ;

☐ an undertaking given on (date) . . . . . by (name of prescribed body) . . . . in the following terms . . . .

The funding of the case has now changed:

☐ the above funding has now ceased

☐ the conditional fee agreement has been terminated

☐ a conditional agreement dated . . . . which provides for a success fee has been entered into

☐ the insurance policy dated . . . . has been cancelled

☐ an insurance policy has been issued by (name of insurer) . . . . on (date) . . . .

☐ the undertaking given on (date) . . . . has been terminated

☐ an undertaking has been given on (date) . . . . by (name of prescribed body) . . . . in the following terms . . . .

Signed . . . . **Date** . . . .
Solicitor for the (claimant)(defendant) (Part 20 defendant) (respondent)(appellant)

The court office at

is open between 10 am and 4 pm Monday to Friday. When corresponding with the court, please address forms or letters to the Court Manager and quote the claim number.
N251 Notice of funding of case or claim (7.00)   The Court Service Publications Unit

10.9 Allocation questionnaire (N150)

Allocation questionnaire

To be completed by, or on behalf of,

	In the
	Claim No.
	Last date for filing with court office

who is [1ʳ][2ⁿᵈ][3ʳᵈ][ ][Claimant][Defendant]
[Part 20 claimant] in this claim

Please read the notes on page five before completing the questionnaire.

You should note the date by which it must be returned and the name of the court it should be returned to since this may be different from the court where the proceedings were issued.

If you have settled this claim (or if you settle it on a future date) and do not need to have it heard or tried, you must let the court know immediately.

Have you sent a copy of this completed form to the other party(ies)? ☐ Yes ☐ No

A Settlement

Do you wish there to be a one month stay to attempt to settle the claim, either by informal discussion or by alternative dispute resolution? ☐ Yes ☐ No

B Location of trial

Is there any reason why your claim needs to be heard at a particular court? ☐ Yes ☐ No

If Yes, say which court and why?

C Pre-action protocols

If an approved pre-action protocol applies to this claim, complete **Part 1** only. If not, complete **Part 2** only. If you answer 'No' to the question in either Part 1 or 2, please explain the reasons why on a separate sheet and attach it to this questionnaire.

Part 1	The' [_____] protocol applies to this claim.		
please say which protocol	Have you complied with it?	☐ Yes	☐ No

Part 2	No pre-action protocol applies to this claim.		
	Have you exchanged information and/or documents (evidence) with the other party in order to assist in settling the claim?	☐ Yes	☐ No

D   Case management information

What amount of the claim is in dispute?   £ [   ]

Applications

Have you made any application(s) in this claim?   ☐ Yes   ☐ No

If Yes, what for? [   ]   For hearing on [   ]
(e.g. summary judgment,
add another party)

Witnesses

So far as you know at this stage, what witnesses of fact do you intend to call at the trial or final hearing including, if appropriate, yourself?

Witness name	Witness to which facts

Experts

Do you wish to use expert evidence at the trial or final hearing?   ☐ Yes   ☐ No

Have you already copied any experts' report(s) to the other party(ies)?   ☐ None yet obtained   ☐ Yes   ☐ No

Do you consider the case suitable for a single joint expert in any field?   ☐ Yes   ☐ No

Please list any single joint experts you propose to use and any other experts you wish to rely on. Identify single joint experts with the initials 'SJ' after their name(s).

Expert's name	Field of expertise (eg orthopaedic surgeon, surveyor, engineer)

Do you want your expert(s) to give evidence orally at the trial or final hearing?   ☐ Yes   ☐ No

If Yes, give the reasons why you think oral evidence is necessary:

2   continue over ▐▐➡

Track

Which track do you consider is most suitable for your claim? Tick one box

☐ small claims track ☐ fast track ☐ multi-track

If you have indicated a track which would not be the normal track for the claim, please give brief reasons for your choice

E Trial or final hearing

How long do you estimate the trial or final hearing will take? ____days ____hours ____minutes

Are there any days when you, an expert or an essential witness will not be able to attend court for the trial or final hearing? ☐ Yes ☐ No

If Yes, please give details

Name	Dates not available

F Proposed directions *(Parties should agree directions wherever possible)*

Have you attached a list of the directions you think appropriate for the management of the claim? ☐ Yes ☐ No

If Yes, have they been agreed with the other party(ies)? ☐ Yes ☐ No

G Costs

Do not complete this section if you have suggested your case is suitable for the small claims track or you have suggested one of the other tracks and you do not have a solicitor acting for you.

What is your estimate of your costs incurred to date? £

What do you estimate your overall costs are likely to be? £

In substantial cases these questions should be answered in compliance with CPR Part 43

3

H Other information

Have you attached documents to this questionnaire? ☐ Yes ☐ No

Have you sent these documents to the other party(ies)? ☐ Yes ☐ No

If Yes, when did they receive them? [   ]

Do you intend to make any applications in the immediate future? ☐ Yes ☐ No

If Yes, what for? [   ]

In the space below, set out any other information you consider will help the judge to manage the claim.

[   ]

Signed [   ]   Date [   ]

[Counsel] [Solicitor] [for the] [1ˢᵗ] [2ⁿᵈ] [3ʳᵈ] [   ]
[Claimant] [Defendant] [Part 20 claimant]

Please enter your firm's name, reference number and full postal address including (if appropriate) details of DX, fax or e-mail

		if applicable
	fax no.	
	DX no.	
Tel. no. Postcode	e-mail	
Your reference no.		

4

Notes for completing an allocation questionnaire

- If the claim is not settled, a judge must allocate it to an appropriate case management track. To help the judge choose the most just and cost-effective track, you must now complete the attached questionnaire.
- If you fail to return the allocation questionnaire by the date given, the judge may make an order which leads to your claim or defence being struck out, or hold an allocation hearing. If there is an allocation hearing the judge may order any party who has not filed their questionnaire to pay, immediately, the costs of that hearing.
- Use a separate sheet if you need more space for your answers marking clearly which section the information refers to. You should write the claim number on it, and on any other documents you send with your allocation questionnaire. Please ensure they are firmly attached to it.
- The letters below refer to the sections of the questionnaire and tell you what information is needed.

A Settlement
If you think that you and the other party may be able to negotiate a settlement you should tick the 'Yes' box. The court may order a stay, whether or not all the other parties to the claim agree. You should still complete the rest of the questionnaire, even if you are requesting a stay. Where a stay is granted it will be for an initial period of one month. You may settle the claim either by informal discussion with the other party or by alternative dispute resolution (ADR). ADR covers a range of different processes which can help settle disputes. More information is available in the booklet 'Resolving Disputes Without Going To Court' available from every county court office.

B Location of trial
High Court cases are usually heard at the Royal Courts of Justice or certain Civil Trial Centres. Fast or multi-track trials may be dealt with at a Civil Trial Centre or at the court where the claim is proceeding. Small claims cases are usually heard at the court in which they are proceeding.

C Pre-action protocols
Before any claim is started, the court expects you to have exchanged information and documents relevant to the claim, to assist in settling it. For some types of claim e.g. personal injury, there are approved protocols that should have been followed.

D Case management information
Applications
It is important for the court to know if you have already made any applications in the claim, what they are for and when they will be heard. The outcome of the applications may affect the case management directions the court gives.

Witnesses
Remember to include yourself as a witness of fact, if you will be giving evidence.

Experts
Oral or written expert evidence will only be allowed at the trial or final hearing with the court's permission. The judge will decide what permission it seems

appropriate to give when the claim is allocated to track. Permission in small claims track cases will only be given exceptionally.

Track
The basic guide by which claims are normally allocated to a track is the amount in dispute, although other factors such as the complexity of the case will also be considered. A leaflet available from the court office explains the limits in greater detail.

Small Claims track	Disputes valued at not more than £5,000 except · those including a claim for personal injuries worth over £1,000 and · those for housing disrepair where either the cost of repairs or other work exceeds £1,000 or any other claim for damages exceeds £1,000
Fast track	Disputes valued at more than £5,000 but not more than £15,000
Multi-track	Disputes over £15,000

E Trial or final hearing
You should enter only those dates when you, your expert(s) or essential witness(es) will not be able to attend court because of holiday or other commitments.

F Proposed directions
Attach the list of directions, if any, you believe will be appropriate to be given for the management of the claim. Agreed directions on fast and multi-track cases should be based on the forms of standard directions set out in the practice direction to CPR Part 28 and form PF52.

G Costs
Only complete this section if you are a solicitor and have suggested the claim is suitable for allocation to the fast or multi-track.

H Other information
Answer the questions in this section. Decide if there is any other information you consider will help the judge to manage the claim. Give details in the space provided referring to any documents you have attached to support what you are saying.

10.10 Application notice (N244)

Application Notice

	In the
You should provide this information for listing the application	

You should provide this information for listing the application
1. How do you wish to have your application dealt with

a) at a hearing? ☐ } *complete all questions below*
b) at a telephone conference? ☐
c) without a hearing? ☐ *complete Qs 3 and 6 below*

2. Give a time estimate for the hearing/conference
_____ (hours) _____ (mins)

3. Is this agreed by all parties? ☐ Yes ☐ No

4. Give dates of any trial period or fixed trial date _____

5. Level of judge _____

6. Parties to be served _____

In the	
Claim no.	
Warrant no. (if applicable)	
Claimant (including ref)	
Defendant(s) (including ref)	
Date	

Note You must complete Parts A **and** B, **and** Part C if applicable. Send any relevant fee and the completed application to the court with any draft order, witness statement or other evidence; and sufficient copies for service on each respondent.

Part A

1. Enter your full name, or name of solicitor
I (We)[1]

(on behalf of)(the claimant)(the defendant)

2. State clearly what order you are seeking and if possible attach a draft
intend to apply for an order (a draft of which is attached) that[2]

because[3]

3. Briefly set out why you are seeking the order. Include the material facts on which you rely, identifying any rule or statutory provision.

Part B

I (We) wish to rely on: *tick one box*

the attached (witness statement)(affidavit) ☐   my statement of case ☐

4. If you are not already a party to the proceedings, you must provide an address for service of documents.

evidence in Part C in support of my application ☐

Signed _____   **Position or office held** _____
(Applicant)('s Solicitor)('s litigation friend)   (if signing on behalf of firm or company)

Address to which documents about this claim should be sent (including reference if appropriate)[4]

			if applicable
		fax no.	
		DX no.	
Tel. no.	Postcode	e-mail	

The court office at

is open from 10 am to 4 pm Monday to Friday. When corresponding with the court please address forms or letters to the Court Manager and quote the claim number.

Part C   Claim No. [   ]

I (We) wish to rely on the following evidence in support of this application:

Statement of Truth

*(I believe) *(The applicant believes) that the facts stated in Part C are true

delete as appropriate

Signed [   ]   **Position or office held** [   ]

(Applicant)('s Solicitor)('s litigation friend)   (if signing on behalf of firm or company)

                                        Date [   ]

10.11 Notice of payment into court (N242A)

Notice of Payment into court
(in settlement - Part 36)

In the	
Claim No.	
Claimant (including ref)	
Defendant (including ref)	

To the Claimant ('s Solicitor)

Take notice the defendant _____ has paid £ _____ (a further amount of £ _____)
into court in settlement of
(tick as appropriate)

☐ the whole of your claim

☐ part of your claim *(give details below)*

☐ a certain issue or issues in your claim *(give details below)*

The (part) (issue or issues) to which it relates is (are):*(give details)*

☐ It is in addition to the amount of £_____ already paid into court on_____ and the total amount in court now offered in settlement is £_____ *(give total of all payments in court to date.)*

☐ It is not inclusive of interest and an additional amount of £_____ is offered for interest *(give details of the rate(s) and period(s) for which the amount of interest is offered.)*

☐ It takes into account all(part) of the following counterclaim:*(give details of the party and the part of the counterclaim to which the payment relates)*

☐ It takes into account the interim payment(s) made in the following amount(s) on the following date(s): *(give details)*

Note: This notice will need to be modified where an offer of provisional damages is made (CPR Part 36.7) and/or where it is made in relation to a mixed (money and non-money) claim in settlement of the whole claim (CPR Part 36.4).

N242A Notice of payment into court (in settlement) (12.99)   The Court Service Publications Unit

For cases where the Social Security (Recovery of Benefits) Act 1997 applies

The gross amount of the compensation payment is £ _____

The defendant has reduced this sum by £_____ in accordance with section 8 of and Schedule 2 to the Social Security (Recovery of Benefits) Act 1997, which was calculated as follows:

    Type of benefit   Amount

The amount paid into court is the net amount after deduction of the amount of benefit.

Signed

Defendant('s solicitor)

Position held
(If signing on
behalf of a firm
or company)

Date

10.12 List of documents (N265)

List of documents: standard disclosure

Notes
- The rules relating to standard disclosure are contained in Part 31 of the Civil Procedure Rules.
- Documents to be included under standard disclosure are contained in Rule 31.6
- A document has or will have been in your control if you have or have had possession, or a right of possession, of it or a right to inspect or take copies of it.

In the	
Claim No.	
Claimant (including ref)	
Defendant (including ref)	
Date	

Disclosure Statement

I state that I have carried out a reasonable and proportionate search to locate all the documents which I am required to disclose under the order made by the court on (insert date)

(I did not search for documents-

1.   pre-dating

2.   located elsewhere than

3.   in categories other than

)

I certify that I understand the duty of disclosure and to the best of my knowledge I have carried out that duty. I further certify that the list of documents set out in or attached to this form, is a complete list of all documents which are or have been in my control and which I am obliged under the order to disclose.

I understand that I must inform the court and the other parties immediately if any further document required to be disclosed by Rule 31.6 comes into my control at any time before the conclusion of the case.

(I have not permitted inspection of documents within the category or class of documents (as set out below) required to be disclosed under Rule 31 (h)(b) or (c) on the grounds that to do so would be disproportionate to the issues in the case.)

Signed _____   Date _____

(Claimant)(Defendant)('s litigation friend)

Position or office held (if signing on behalf of firm or company)
Please state why you are the appropriate person to make the disclosure statement.

List of documents
N265 - w3 standard disclosure (4.99)

continued overleaf
Printed on behalf of The Court Service

List and number here, in a consecutive order, the documents (or bundles of documents if of the same nature, e.g. invoices) in your control, which you do not object to being inspected. Give a short description of each document or bundle so that it can be identified, and say if it is kept elsewhere i.e. with a bank or solicitor

I have control of the documents numbered and listed here. I do not object to you inspecting them/producing copies.

List and number here, as above, the documents in your control which you object to being inspected. (Rule 31.19)

I have control of the documents numbered and listed here, but I object to you inspecting them.

Say what your objections are

I object to you inspecting these documents because:

List and number here, the documents you once had in your control, but which you no longer have. For each document listed, say when it was last in your control and where it is now.

I have had the documents numbered and listed below, but they are no longer in my control.

10.13 Listing questionnaire (N170)

Listing questionnaire

In the

Claim No.

Last date for filing
with court office

To

- The court will use the information which you and the other party(ies) provide to fix a date for trial (or to confirm the date and time if one has already been fixed), to confirm the estimated length of trial and to set a timetable for the trial itself. In multi-track cases the court will also decide whether to hold a pre-trial review.
- If you do not complete and return the questionnaire the procedural judge may
    - make an order which leads to your statement of case (claim or defence) being struck out.
    - decide to hold a listing hearing. You may be ordered to pay (immediately) the other parties' costs of attending.
    - if there is sufficient information, list the case for trial and give any appropriate directions.
- Separate estimates of costs incurred to date and those which will be incurred if the case proceeds to trial, should be given using Form 1 in the Schedule of Costs Forms set out in the Civil Procedure Rules. This form should be attached to and returned with your completed questionnaire. (This relates only to costs incurred by legal representatives.)

A Directions complied with

1. Have you complied with all the previous directions given by the court?   Yes   No

2. If no, please explain which directions are outstanding and why

Directions outstanding	Reasons directions outstanding

3. Are any further directions required to prepare the case for trial?   Yes   No
(If no go to section B)

4. If yes, please explain directions required and give reasons

Directions required	Reasons required

B Experts

1. Has the court already given permission for you to use written expert evidence? ☐ Yes ☐ No *(If no go to section B6)*

2. If yes, please give name and field of expertise.

Name of expert	Whether joint expert (please tick, if appropriate)	Field of expertise

3. Have the expert(s') report(s) been agreed with the other parties? ☐ Yes ☐ No

4. Have the experts met to discuss their reports? ☐ Yes ☐ No

5. Has the court already given permission for the expert(s) to give oral evidence at the trial? *(If yes go to Q8)* ☐ Yes ☐ No

6. If no, are you seeking that permission? *(If yes go to Q7)* ☐ Yes ☐ No *(If no go to section C)*

7. Give your reasons for seeking permission.

8. What are the names, addresses and fields of expertise of your experts?

Expert 1	Expert 2	Expert 3	Expert 4

9. Please give details of any dates within the trial period when your expert(s) will not be available.

Name of expert	Dates not available

C Other witnesses

(If you are not calling other witnesses go to section D)

1. How many other witnesses (including yourself) will be giving evidence on your behalf at the trial? (do not include experts - see section B above)

(Give number)

2. What are the names and addresses of your witnesses?

Witness 1	Witness 2	Witness 3	Witness 4

3. Please give details of any dates within the trial period when you or your witnesses will not be available?

Name of witness	Dates not available

4. Are any of the witness statements agreed?   Yes   No
(If no go to Q6)

5. If yes, give the name of the witness and the date of his or her statement

Name of witness	Date of statement

6. Do you or any of your witnesses need any special facilities?   Yes   No
(If no go to Q8)

7. If yes, what are they?

8. Will any of your witnesses be provided with an interpreter?   Yes   No
(If no go to section D)

9. If yes, say what type of interpreter e.g. language (stating which), deaf/blind etc.

D Legal representation

1. Who will be presenting your case at the hearing or trial?   You   Solicitor   Counsel

2. Please give details of any dates within the trial period when the person presenting your case will not be available.

Name	Dates not available

E Other matters

1. How long do you estimate the trial will take, including cross-examination and closing arguments?

Minutes	Hours	Days

If your case is allocated to the fast track the maximum time allowed for the whole case will be no more than one day.

2. What is the estimated number of pages of evidence to be included in the trial bundle?

(please give number)

Fast track cases only

3. The court will normally give you 3 weeks notice in the fast track of the date fixed for a fast track trial unless, in exceptional circumstances, the court directs that shorter notice will be given. Would you be prepared to accept shorter notice of the date fixed for trial?   Yes   No

Signed

Claimant/defendant or Counsel/Solicitor for the claimant/defendant

Date

10.14 Statement of costs (N260)

**Statement of Costs
(summary assessment)**

In the	
	Court
Case Reference	

Judge/Master

Case Title

[Party]'s Statement of Costs for the hearing on *(date)*   (interim application/fast track trial)

Description of fee earners*
  (a) *(name) (grade) (hourly rate claimed)*
  (b) *(name) (grade) (hourly rate claimed)*

Attendances on   *(party)*
  (a) *(number)*   hours at £   £
  (b) *(number)*   hours at £   £

Attendances on opponents
  (a) *(number)*   hours at £   £
  (b) *(number)*   hours at £   £

Attendance on others
  (a) *(number)*   hours at £   £
  (b) *(number)*   hours at £   £

Site inspections etc
  (a) *(number)*   hours at £   £
  (b) *(number)*   hours at £   £

Work done on negotiations
  (a) *(number)*   hours at £   £
  (b) *(number)*   hours at £   £

Other work, not covered above
  (a) *(number)*   hours at £   £
  (b) *(number)*   hours at £   £

Work done on documents
  (a) *(number)*   hours at £   £
  (b) *(number)*   hours at £   £

Attendance at hearing
  (a) *(number)*   hours at £   £
  (b) *(number)*   hours at £   £
  (a) *(number)*   hours travel and waiting at £   £
  (b) *(number)*   hours travel and waiting at £   £

Sub Total £

Brought forward £ [_____]

Counsel's fees *(name) (year of call)* [_____]

    Fee for [advice/conference/documents] £ [_____]

    Fee for hearing £ [_____]

Other expenses

    [court fees] £ [_____]

    Others £ [_____]

    (give brief description) [_____]

    Total £ [_____]

    Amount of VAT claimed

        on solicitors and counsel's fees £ [_____]

        on other expenses £ [_____]

    Grand Total £ [_____]

The costs estimated above do not exceed the costs which the *(party)* [_____] is liable to pay in respect of the work which this estimate covers.

Dated [_____]   Signed [_____]

Name of firm of solicitors [partner] for the *(party)* [_____]

---

* 4 grades of fee earner are suggested:

(A) Solicitors with over eight years post qualification experience including at least eight years litigation experience.

(B) Solicitors and legal executives with over four years post qualification experience including at least four years litigation experience.

(C) Other solicitors and legal executives and fee earners of equivalent experience.

(D) Trainee solicitors, para legals and other fee earners.

"Legal Executive" means a Fellow of the Institute of Legal Executives. Those who are not Fellows of the Institute are not entitled to call themselves legal executives and in principle are therefore not entitled to the same hourly rate as a legal executive.

In respect of each fee earner communications should be treated as attendances and routine communications should be claimed at one tenth of the hourly rate.

11 Summary of Procedure

11.1 Determining the value of a claim

(a) No account is taken of any possible finding of contributory negligence – unless that negligence is admitted.

(b) No account is taken of interest.

(c) If the claimant is seeking an award for provisional damages, no account will be taken of the possibility of a future application for such damages.

(d) Costs are not taken into account.

(e) Moneys liable to recoupment by the DSS are taken into account.

11.2 The small claims track

The small claims track limit is now governed by the issue of whether or not general damages for pain and suffering exceeds £1,000. It is necessary to state that the claim for pain and suffering exceeds this figure.

11.2.1 Where the claim can be issued

A personal injury action can be launched in any county court. When the defendant files an acknowledgement of service he can apply to have the action transferred to his home court. Furthermore, either party may apply to the court where the claim is proceeding for the transfer of proceedings to another court under Civil Procedure Rule 30.2 or may specify their preferred court in the allocation questionnaire.

11.2.2 Drafting the particulars of claim

The claim form must clearly state the value of the claim. The purpose of this is to enable the court to allocate the claim to the relevant track. The small claims track is for claims for personal injury valued at less than £1,000, total damages sought not to exceed £5,000. The fast track is the usual track for claims where damages for the personal injury have a value of more than £5,000 but the total value of the claim is less than £15,000 and the multitrack is for claims over £15,000.

11.2.3 Service

If the court does not serve proceedings, the claimant's solicitor must serve the claim form and particulars of claim within four months after the date of issue of the claim form. The claim form may be served by post; particular care must be taken to ensure that service takes place at the nominated address for service or on the nominated solicitor.

11.2.4 Documents to be served with the particulars of claim

The following documents must accompany the particulars of claim:

(a) a medical report;

(b) a statement of the special damages claimed.

11.3   Case management directions

When the defendant files a defence the court will serve an allocation questionnaire on each party. Once the allocation questionnaires have been filed, or the time for filing has expired, the court will allocate a claim to a track and will serve notice of allocation on every party.

11.3.1 Fast track directions

On allocation to the fast track, the court will fix a trial date and tailor its directions to individual cases. A timetable will be set for those steps to be taken. Directions will include:

(a) disclosure (usually standard, although the court may direct that no disclosure is to take place or specify the class of documents to be disclosed);

(b) service of witness statements; and

(c) expert evidence.

A typical timetable from the date of notice of allocation the court may give for preparation of the case is as follows:

Disclosure	4 weeks
Exchange of witness statements	10 weeks
Exchange of experts' reports	14 weeks
Sending of listing questionnaires by the court	20 weeks
Filing of completed listing questionnaires	22 weeks
Hearing	30 weeks

11.3.2 Multitrack directions

On allocation to the multitrack, the court will give case management directions and a timetable for those steps to be taken. The court will also fix a case management conference or a pre-trial review or both, as well as fixing a trial date or period in which the trial is to take place. The essence of the multitrack is flexibility and, as such, there are no specimen or standard directions. This track deals with claims of higher value, claims which cannot be dealt with in one day and complex claims. Where the claim is not complex the court will give similar directions to those applied in fast track claims.

Directions the court must give on listing are:

(a) the court must fix a trial date or week, give a time estimate and fix the place;

(b) the parties should seek to agree directions and may file an agreed order. The court may make an order in those terms or it may make a different order;

(c) agreed directions should include provision about –

- evidence, especially expert evidence;
- a trial timetable and a time estimate;
- the preparation of a trial bundle;
- any other matter needed to prepare the case for trial.

11.4 Preparing a bundle for trial

The parties should receive at least 21 days' notice of the hearing. Where possible, the parties should agree the contents of the bundle. Not more than seven days and not less than three days before the start of the trial, the claimant must file the trial bundle, which must be paginated, indexed and contained in a ring binder. The bundle should include the claim form and all statements of case, witness statements, requests for further and better particulars and experts' reports. Identical bundles should be supplied to all the parties to the proceedings and for the use of witnesses.

12 Matters Requiring Special Care

This chapter deals with three matters requiring special care: the drafting of witness statements, cases involving the Motor Insurers Bureau and the Pre-Action Protocol for the Resolution of Clinical Disputes.

12.1 Drafting witness statements

The drafting of the witness statement is isolated here because it is an essential part of the personal injury process that is often overlooked.

- It is extremely difficult, at trial, to repair the damage caused by bad witness statements.
- Witness statements can create insurmountable problems and lose a case.
- Effective witness statements can serve to win the case.

The rules

The rules relating to witness statements are at Part 32 of the Civil Procedure Rules and are supplemented by a very important Practice Direction.

The form of a witness statement

Paragraph 17 of the Practice Direction that accompanies Part 32 states that:

- The witness statement should be headed with the title of the proceedings. Where the proceedings are between several parties with the same status it is possible to truncate the heading.

- At the top right hand corner of the first page there should be clearly written:
  - o the party on whose behalf it is made;
  - o the initials and surname of the witness;
  - o the number of the statement in relation to that witness;
  - o the identifying initials and number of each exhibit referred to; and
  - o the date the statement was made.

The body of the witness statement

Paragraph 18 of the Practice Direction states:

18.1 The witness statement must, if practicable, be in the intended witness's own words. The statement should be expressed in the first person and should also state:

1   the full name of the witness.

2   his place of residence or, if he is making the statement in his professional, business or other occupational capacity, the address at which he works, the position he holds and the name of his firm or employer,

3   his occupation, or if he has none, his description.

4   the fact that he is a party to the proceedings or is the employee of such a party if it be the case.

18.2 A witness statement must indicate:

1   which of the statements in it are made from the witness's own knowledge and which are matters of information or belief.

2   the source for any matters of information or belief.

18.3 An exhibit used in conjunction with a witness statement should be verified and identified by the witness and remain separate from the witness statement.

18.4 Where a witness refers to an exhibit or exhibits he should state 'I refer to the (description of exhibit) marked ...'

18.5 The provisions of paragraphs 11.3 to 15.3 [Exhibits] apply similarly to witness statements as they do to affidavits. [A later article will deal with the rules relating to exhibits.]

18.6 Where a witness makes more than one witness statement to which there are exhibits, in the same action, the numbering of the exhibits should run consecutively throughout and not start again with each witness statement.

The format of witness statements

It is important that litigators are aware of the precise format required of witness statements (a failure to comply with the requirements can lead to the evidence not being admitted or the costs of preparation being disallowed).

19.1 A witness statement must:

1   be produced on durable quality A4 paper with a 3.5cm margin,

2   be fully legible and should normally be typed on one side of the paper only,

3   where possible, be bound securely in a manner which would not hamper filing, or otherwise each page should be indorsed with the case number and should bear the initials of the witness,

4   have the pages numbered consecutively as a separate statement (or one of several statements contained in a file),

5   be divided into numbered paragraphs,

6   have all numbers, including dates, expressed in figures,

7   give in the margin the reference to any document or documents mentioned.

19.2 It is usually convenient for a witness statement to follow the chronological sequence of the events or matters dealt with. Each paragraph of a witness statement should as far as possible be confined to a distinct portion of the subject.

20.1 A witness statement is the equivalent of the oral evidence which the witness would, if called, give in his evidence in chief at the trial; it must include a statement by the intended witness that he believes the facts in it are true.

20.2 To verify a witness statement the statement of truth is as follows:

I believe that the facts stated in this witness statement are true.

20.3 Attention is drawn to rule 32.14 which sets out the consequences of verifying a witness statement containing a false statement without an honest belief in its truth.' (It is a contempt of court).

The basic point for present purposes is that the *structure* of the statement must be correct. A statement that does not comply with the rules may not be admitted and, due to no fault of the witness, may be given less weight.

Use of precedents

Individual styles of drafting vary; however, it is important that:

(1) The statements are in a logical order with numbered paragraphs.

(2) All the matters that the party needs to establish (or disprove) are dealt with.

Preparation for drafting

1 Read the statements of case.

Know what is in issue. Particularly any positive allegations, contributory negligence, failure to mitigate loss.

2 Read the documents.

Have you seen all the defendant's documents? Are there any that present any real difficulties? Can you explain these difficulties?

3 Go back to basics.

Think again what you have to achieve. How does each sentence in the witness statement progress towards this? Is there any unnecessary material (eg personal abuse) that can be excluded?

12.2   Dealing with the Motor Insurers Bureau

A new MIB agreement for dealing with uninsured drivers came into force on 1 October 1999. This places onerous duties on claimant lawyers.

Conditions precedent to MIB's liability

The agreement states that the MIB shall incur no liability unless application is made to the person specified in clause 9(1):

* in such form;
* giving such information about the relevant proceedings and other matters relevant to the agreement; and
* accompanied by such documents as MIB may reasonably require.

Service of notices on the MIB

Notice will *only* be sufficiently given if by fax or by registered or recorded delivery to the MIB's registered office. Delivery shall be proved by the production of a fax transmission report produced by the sender's facsimile machine or an appropriate postal receipt.

Clause 9 of the agreement: the need to give proper notice

Clause 9(1) states that the MIB shall not incur liability unless proper notice is given within 14 days of the commencement of proceedings (in cases where an insurer with a relevant interest can be identified) to that insurer, or in any other case to the MIB.

'Proper notice'

Take careful note of the matters that you are required to produce to show 'proper notice':

* Notice in writing that proceedings have been issued by claim form, writ or other means.
* A copy of the sealed claim form, writ or other official documents providing evidence of the commencement of the proceedings.
* A copy or details of any insurance policy providing benefits in the case of the death, bodily injury or damage to property to which the proceedings relate where the claimant is the insured party and the benefits are available to him.

- Copies of all correspondence in the possession of the claimant or his solicitor or agent to or from the Defendant, his solicitor or agents which is relevant to:
    - The death, bodily injury or damage for which the Defendant is alleged to be responsible.
    - Any contract of insurance which covers, or which may or which has been alleged to cover, liability for such death, injury or damage the benefit of which is, or is claimed to be, available to the Defendant.
- A copy of the particulars of claim, whether served or not.
- A copy of all other documents which are required under the appropriate rules of procedure to be served on the defendant with the claim form, writ or other originating process or with the particulars of claim.
- Such other information about the relevant proceedings as MIB may reasonably specify.

Clause 9(3) states:

> If in the case of proceedings commenced in England or Wales, the Particulars of Claim (including any document required to be served therewith) has not yet been served with the Claim Form or other originating process paragraph (2)(e) shall be sufficiently complied with if a copy thereof is served on MIB not later than seven days after it is served on the Defendant.

Notice of service of proceedings

Note that there are two obligations:
- To give notice of issue.
- To give notice of service.

Clause 10(2) states that the MIB will not incur liability unless notice, in writing, is given within seven days of service. That is seven days after:
- The date when the Defendant received notification from the Court that service has occurred.
- The date when the claimant receives notification from the Defendant that service of the claim form or other originating process has occurred.
- The date of personal service.

Or 'the appropriate date' can mean:
* 14 days after the date when service is deemed to have occurred in accordance with the Civil Procedure Rules,

whichever of these dates occurs first.

Yet more information

The MIB is not liable unless the claimant, within seven days of any of the following events, gives notice to the MIB or insurer concerned:
* The filing of a defence.
* Any amendment of the particulars of claim or any amendment of or addition to any schedule or other document required to be served therewith; and
* Either the setting down of the action or, where the court gives notice to the claimant of the trial date, the date when that notice is received.

The MIB must also be sent copies of the documents within seven days.

NOTE: the requirement to file documents could be construed to include supplementary letters from doctors.

A 'catch-all'

Clause 11(2) states that the MIB shall not incur any liability unless the claimant (which includes his solicitors) furnishes such further information and documents in support of the claim as the MIB may reasonably require. *Notwithstanding* that the claimant may have complied with all the earlier obligations.

Applying for judgment

Clause 12 states that the MIB shall incur no liability unless the claimant has, after commencement of the proceedings, and not less than 35 days before the appropriate date, given notice in writing of his intention to apply for judgment.

Clause 13

Again, this states that the MIB shall not be liable unless the claimant has *as soon as reasonably practicable* demand the information specified in s 154(1) of the Road Traffic Act 1988 (ie, a request to give particulars of insurance). If the person of whom demand is made fails to comply with the provisions of s 154, a formal complaint must be made to a police officer and the name and address of the registered keeper of the vehicle should be obtained.

Duty to pursue other parties

Clause 14(1) states that the MIB shall incur no liability under MIB's obligation unless the claimant has, if so required by the MIB (and upon the MIB giving an indemnity as to costs), taken all reasonable steps to obtain judgment against every person who may be liable (including any person who may be vicariously liable) in respect of the claim.

Do not refuse to consent

Similarly, clause 14(2) states that the MIB shall incur no liability if the claimant, upon being requested to do so by MIB, refuses to consent to MIB being joined as a defendant to the relevant proceedings.

Assignment of judgment and undertakings

Clause 15 states that the MIB shall incur no liability unless the claimant has assigned to the MIB or its nominee the unsatisfied judgment and undertaken to repay to the MIB any sums paid to him subsequently received.

Compensation received from other sources

Clause 17 states that where a claimant has received compensation from the Policyholders Protection Board or an insurer under an agreement or arrangement or any other source in respect of the death, bodily injury or other damage to which the relevant proceedings relate and such compensation has not been taken into account in the calculation of the relevant sum, the MIB may deduct from the relevant sum an amount equal to that compensation.

The need to be careful

The above requirements are set out in some detail to ensure that litigators are fully aware of the potential problems.

Further reading

See *APIL Guide to the MIB* (2001, Jordans).

12.3 The Clinical Negligence Protocol

Because of the particular requirements of this Protocol, these requirements are set out in some detail.

Obtaining the health records

Requests for copies of the patient's clinical records should be made using the Law Society and the Department of Health approved standard forms, adapted as necessary. The copy records should be provided within 40 days of the request and for a cost not exceeding that permissible under the Access to Health Records Act 1990. If the healthcare provider fails to provide the records within 40 days, the patient or adviser can then apply to the court for an order for pre-action disclosure. The court also has the power to impose costs sanctions for unreasonable delay in providing records.

Letter of claim

Following receipt and analysis of the records, if there is grounds for a claim, the claimant should send, as soon as is practicable, a letter of claim. The letter should contain a clear summary of the facts on which the claim is based, including the alleged adverse outcome and the main allegations of negligence. It should also describe the patient's injuries and outline the financial loss incurred by the claimant with an indication of the heads of damage to be claimed, unless this is impossible. In more complex cases, a chronology of the relevant events should be provided. The letter of claim should also refer to relevant documents and, if possible, enclose copies of any which will not already be in the defendant's possession. Sufficient information must be given to enable the defendant to commence investigations. It should be noted that letters of claim and the subsequent statement of claim in the proceedings can differ without necessarily incurring sanctions.

Proceedings

Proceedings should not be issued until after three months from the letter of claim, unless there is a limitation problem or the patient's position needs to be protected by early issue.

Offer to settle

The patient or their adviser may make an offer to settle the claim at this early stage by putting forward an amount of compensation which would be satisfactory.

The response

The defendant should acknowledge the letter of claim within 14 days of receipt and should identify the person dealing with the matter.

The defendant should within three months of the letter of claim provide a reasoned answer. If the claim is admitted, this should be stated in clear terms. Where only part of the claim is admitted, it should be made clear which issues of breach and/or causation are admitted and which are denied and why.

If the claim is denied, this should include specific comments on the allegations of negligence and if a chronology of relevant events has been provided and is disputed, the defendant must set out his version of events.

Where additional documents are relied on, such as internal protocols, copies should be provided.

Offer to settle

Where the claimant has made an offer to settle the defendant should respond to that offer, preferably with reasons. The defendant may make an offer of their own to settle at this stage either as a counter-offer or of their own accord, but should accompany any offer with supporting medical evidence and/or evidence in relation to the value of the claim which is in the defendant's possession.

Agreement on liability

Where the parties agree on liability but time is needed to resolve the value of the claim, they should aim to agree a reasonable period.

13 Further Reading

Substantive law

Andrews and Lee, *Catastrophic Injuries: A Practical Guide to Compensation*, 1997, Sweet & Maxwell

Barrett and Howells, *Cases and Materials on Occupational Health and Safety Law*, 2nd edn, 2000, Cavendish Publishing

Bingham, *Motor Claims Cases*, 11th edn, 2001, Butterworths

Carey, *Tripping and Slipping*, 1997, EMIS Professional

Clerk and Lindsell on Torts, Brazier *et al*, 17th edn, 1995, Sweet & Maxwell

Foster, *Tripping and Slipping Cases: A Practitioner's Guide*, 2nd edn, 1996, Sweet & Maxwell

Harpwood, *Principles of Tort Law*, 4th edn, 2000, Cavendish Publishing

Holyoak and Allen, *Civil Liability for Defective Premises*, 1982, Butterworths

Jackson and Powell, *Professional Negligence*, 2nd edn, 1987, Sweet & Maxwell

Kemp, *Damages for Personal Injury and Death*, 5th edn, 1993, Longman

Kemp and Kemp, *The Quantum of Damages*, 1975, Sweet & Maxwell (looseleaf)

Khan, Robson and Swift, *Clinical Negligence*, 2nd edn, 2001, Cavendish Publishing

Lewis, *Deducting Benefits from Damages for Personal Injury*, 1999, Oxford University Press

Miller, *Product Safety Encyclopedia*, Butterworths (looseleaf)

Munkman, *Damages for Personal Injuries and Death*, 5th edn, 1996, Butterworths

Munkman, *Employer's Liability*, 12th edn, 1995, Butterworths

Percy (ed), *Charlesworth and Percy on Negligence*, 10th edn, 2001, Sweet & Maxwell

Scott, *The General Practitioner and the Law of Negligence*, 1995, Cavendish Publishing

Smith, Goddard, Killalea and Randall, *Health and Safety: The Modern Legal Framework*, 2nd edn, 2001, Butterworths

Stephenson, *Sourcebook on Torts*, 2nd edn, 2000, Cavendish Publishing

Warren Neocleous, *Personal Injury: Practice and Procedure in Europe*, 1997, Cavendish Publishing

Procedure: general

Blackford and Price, *County Court Practice Handbook*

Bowers and Gatt, *Procedure in Courts and Tribunals,* 2nd edn, 2000, Cavendish Publishing

Hendy, Day, Buchan and Kennedy, *Personal Injury Practice: The Guide to Litigation in the County Courts and the High Court*, 3rd edn, 2000, Butterworths

Humphreys' District Registry Practice, 25th edn, 1991, Longman

Gerlis, *County Court Procedure*, 3rd edn, 2001, Cavendish Publishing

Godrein and De Haas, *Personal Injury Encyclopaedia*, looseleaf, Butterworths

O'Hare and Hill, *Civil Litigation*, 2001, Sweet & Maxwell

Pritchard *et al*, *Personal Injury Litigation*, 2002, Sweet & Maxwell

Professional Negligence Bar Association, *Tables for the Calculation of Damages*, Sweet & Maxwell (annual)

Vindis and Ritchie, *MIB Claims*, 2001, Jordans

Specific aspects

Birks, *Contentious Costs,* 3rd edn, 2001, Cavendish Publishing

Bullen Leake and Jacob, *Precedents of Pleadings,* 14th edn, 2000, Sweet & Maxwell

Butterworth's County Court Precedents and Pleadings (looseleaf)

di Mambro, D, *Manual of Civil Appeals*, 2001, Butterworths

Jones, MA, *Limitation Periods in Personal Injury Actions*, 1995, Blackstone

Spencer, *Legal Aid,* 2nd edn, 1996, Cavendish Publishing

Evidence

Cowsill and Clegg, *Evidence: Law and Practice*

Style and Hollander, *Documentary Evidence*, 2000, Sweet & Maxwell

Fatal accidents

Exall, G, *The APIL Guide to Fatal Accident Claims*, 2002, Jordans

Yelton, M, *Fatal Accidents: A Guide to Compensation*, 1998, Sweet & Maxwell

Journals

Journal of Personal Injury Litigation, Sweet & Maxwell (quarterly)

14 Useful Addresses

Association of Consulting Engineers

Alliance House
12 Caxton Street
London
SW1H 0QL

Tel: 0207 222 6557
Email: consult@acenet.co.uk
Web: www.acenet.co.uk

Action for Victims of Medical Negligence

Bank Chambers
1 London Road
Forest Hill
London
SE23 3TP

Tel: 0208 686 8333

Criminal Injuries Compensation Authority

Tay House
300 Bath Street
Glasgow
G2 4JR

Tel: 0141 331 2726

Web: www.cica.gov.uk

Compensation Recovery Unit

Department of Social Security

Reyrolle Building

Hebburn

Tyne & Wear

NE31 1XB

Tel: 0191 201 0500

HSE Information Centre

Broad Lane

Sheffield

S3 7HQ

Tel: 08701 545500

Email: public.inquiries@hse.gsi.gov.uk

Web: www.hse.gov.uk

Medical Defence Union

3 Devonshire Place

London

W1N 2EA

Tel: 0207 2021500

Email: mdu@v-mdu.com

Web: www.v-mdu.com

Medical Protection Society

35 Cavendish Square
London
W1M 0PS

Tel: 0207 637 0541
Email: info@mts.org.uk
Web: www.mts.org.uk

Motor Insurers' Bureau

152 Silbury Boulevard Central
Milton Keynes
MK9 1NB

Tel: 01908 240000
Fax: 01908 671681
Email: mib.org.uk

Association of Personal Injury Lawyers

33 Pilcher Gate
Nottingham
NG1 1QE

Tel: 0115 958 0585
Email: mail@apil.com
Web: www.apil.com

15 Appendix

PRE-ACTION PROTOCOL LETTER FOR PERSONAL
INJURY CLAIMS

LETTER OF CLAIM

To

Defendant

Dear Sirs

Re: **Claimant's full name**
Claimant's full address
Claimant's Clock or Works Number
Claimant's Employer (*name and address*)

We are instructed by the above named to claim damages in connection
with **an accident at work/ road traffic accident / tripping accident** on
___ day ___ of ___ (*year*) at (*place of accident which must be sufficiently
detailed to establish location*)

Please confirm the identity of your insurers. Please note that the
insurers will need to see this letter as soon as possible and it may affect
your insurance cover and/or the conduct of any subsequent legal
proceedings if you do not send this letter to them.

The circumstances of the accident are:–
(*brief outline*)

The reason why we are alleging fault is:
(*simple explanation e.g. defective machine, broken ground*)

A description of our clients' injuries is as follows:–
(brief outline)

(In cases of road traffic accidents)

Our client (state hospital reference number) received treatment for the injuries at name and address of hospital).

He is employed as *(occupation)* and has had the following time off work *(dates of absence).* His approximate weekly income is *(insert if known).*

If you are our client's employers, please provide us with the usual earnings details which will enable us to calculate his financial loss.

We are obtaining a police report and will let you have a copy of the same upon your undertaking to meet half the fee.

We have also sent a letter of claim to *(name and address)* and a copy of that letter is attached. We understand their insurers are *(name, address and claims number if known).*

At this stage of our enquiries we would expect the documents contained in parts *(insert appropriate parts of standard disclosure list)* to be relevant to this action.

A copy of this letter is attached for you to send to your insurers. Finally we expect an acknowledgement of this letter within 21 days by yourselves or your insurers.

Yours faithfully

PRE-ACTION PROTOCOL FOR PERSONAL INJURY CLAIMS

ANNEX C

LETTER OF INSTRUCTION

Dear Sir,

Re: *(Name and Address)*

D.O.B. –
Telephone No. –
Date of Accident –

We are acting for the above named in connection with injuries received in an accident which occurred on the above date. The main injuries appear to have been **(main injuries).**

We should be obliged if you would examine our Client and let us have a full and detailed report dealing with any relevant pre-accident medical history, the injuries sustained, treatment received and present condition, dealing in particular with the capacity for work and giving a prognosis.

It is central to our assessment of the extent of our Client's injuries to establish the extent and duration of any continuing disability. Accordingly, in the prognosis section we would ask you to specifically comment on any areas of continuing complaint or disability or impact on daily living. If there is such continuing disability you should comment upon the level of suffering or inconvenience caused and, if you are able, give your view as to when or if the complaint or disability is likely to resolve.

Please send our Client an appointment direct for this purpose. Should you be able to offer a cancellation appointment please contact our Client direct. We confirm we will be responsible for your reasonable fees.

We are obtaining the notes and records from our Client's GP and Hospitals attended and will forward them to you when they are to hand / or please request the GP and Hospital records direct and advise that any invoice for the provision of these records should be forwarded to us.

In order to comply with Court Rules we would be grateful if you would insert above your signature a statement that the contents are true to the best of your knowledge and belief.

In order to avoid further correspondence we can confirm that on the evidence we have there is no reason to suspect we may be pursuing a claim against the hospital or its staff.

We look forward to receiving your report within _____ weeks. If you will not be able to prepare your report within this period please telephone us upon receipt of these instructions.

When acknowledging these instructions it would assist if you could give an estimate as to the likely time scale for the provision of your report and also an indication as to your fee.

Yours faithfully

ANNEX 10a

GUIDE TO COUNTY COURT FEES

Schedule 1, Column 1 Number & description of fee (County Court Fees Order 1999 as amended)	Schedule 1, Column 2 Amount of fee
1. Commencement of proceedings 1.1 On the commencement of originating proceedings (including originating proceedings issued after leave to issue is granted) to recover a sum of money, except in Claims Production Centre (CPC) cases, where the sum claimed:	(a) does not exceed £200 . . . . £27 (b) exceeds 200 but not £300 . . . . £38 (c) exceeds £300 but not £400 . . . . £50 (d) exceeds £400 but not £500 . . . . £60 (e) exceeds 500 but not £1,000 . . . . £80 (f) exceeds £1,000 but not £5,000. . . . . £115 (g) exceeds £5,000 but not £15,000. . . . . £230 (h) exceeds £15,000 but not £50,000. . . . . £350 (i) exceeds £50,000 or not limited £500
1.2 On the commencement of originating proceedings to recover a sum of money in CPC cases, where the sum claimed:	(a) does not exceed £200 . . . . £20 (b) exceeds £200 but not £300 . . . . £31

	(c) exceeds £300 but not £400 . . . . £43
	(d) exceeds £400 but not £500 . . . . £53
	(e) exceeds 500 but not £1,000 . . . . £73
	(f) exceeds £1,000 but not £5,000 . . . . £108
	(g) exceeds £5,000 but not £15,000 . . . . £223
	(h) exceeds £15,000 but not £50,000 . . . . £343
	(i) exceeds £50,000 or not limited £493
1.3 On the commencement of originating proceedings for any other remedy or relief (including originating proceedings issued after leave to issue is granted) *Fees 1.1 and 1.3 Recovery of land or goods* Where a claim for money is additional or alternative to a claim for recovery of land or goods, only fee 1.3 shall be payable. *Fees 1.1 and 1.3 Claims other than recovery of land or goods* Where a claim for money is additional to a non money claim (other than a claim for recovery of land or goods) then fee 1.1 shall be payable in addition to fee 1.3. Where a	£120

claim for money is alternative to a non money claim (other than a claim for recovery of land or goods) then fee 1.1 or fee 1.3 shall be payable, whichever is the greater. *Fees 1.1 and 1.3 Generally* Where more than one non money claim is made in the same proceedings, fee 1.3 shall be payable once only, in addition to any fee which may be payable under fee 1.1. Fees 1.1 and 1.3 shall not be payable where fee 1.6(b) or fee 8 apply. *Fees 1.1 and 1.3 Amendment of claim or counterclaim* Where the claim or counterclaim is amended, and the fee paid before amendment is less than that which would have been payable if the document, as amended, had been so drawn in the first instance, the party amending the document shall pay the difference.	
1.4 On the filing of proceedings against a party or parties not named in the originating proceedings Fee 1.4 shall be payable by a defendant who adds or substitutes a party or parties to the proceedings or by a claimant who adds or substitutes a defendant or defendants.	£30

1.5 On the filing of a counterclaim	The same fee as if the relief or remedy sought were the subject of separate proceedings
1.6(a) On an application for leave to issue originating proceedings	£30
(b) On an application for an order under Part III of the Solicitors Act 1974, for the assessment of costs payable to a solicitor by his client or on commencement of costs-only proceedings	£30
2. General Fees	
2.1 On the claimant filing an allocation questionnaire; or • Where the court dispenses with the need for an allocation questionnaire, within 14 days of the date of despatch of the notice of allocation to track; or • where the CPR or a Practice Direction provide for automatic allocation or provide that the rules on allocation shall not apply, within 28 days of the filing of the defence (or the filing of the last defence if there is more than one defendant), or within 28 days of the expiry of the time permitted for filing all defences if sooner	£80

Fee 2.1 shall be payable by the claimant except where the action is proceeding on the counterclaim alone, when it shall be payable by the defendant – • on the defendant filing an allocation questionnaire; or • where the court dispenses with the need for an allocation questionnaire, within 14 days of the date of despatch of the notice of allocation to track; or • where the CPR or a Practice Direction provide for automatic allocation or provide that the rules on allocation shall not apply, within 28 days of the filing of the defence to the counterclaim (or the filing of the last defence to the counterclaim if there is more than one party entitled to file a defence to a counterclaim), or within 28 days of the expiry of the time permitted for filing all defences to the counterclaim if sooner	
2.2 On the claimant filing a listing questionnaire; or • where the court fixes the trial date or trial week without the need for a listing questionnaire, within 14 days of the date of despatch of the notice (or the date when oral notice is given if no written	

notice is given) of the trial week or the trial date if no trial week is fixed:	
(a) if the case is on the multi-track	£300
(b) in any other case	£200
Fee 2.2 shall be payable by the claimant except where the action is proceeding on the counterclaim alone, when it shall be payable by the defendant – • on the defendant filing a listing questionnaire; or • where the court fixes the trial date or trial week without the need for a listing questionnaire, within 14 days of the date of despatch of the notice (or the date when oral notice is given if no written notice is given) of the trial week or the trial date if no trial week is fixed	
Where the court receives notice in writing - • before the trial date has been fixed or, • where a trial date has been fixed, at least 7 days before the trial date,	

from the party who paid fee 2.2 that the case is settled or discontinued, fee 2.2 shall be refunded.	
Fees 2.1 and 2.2 Generally Fees 2.1 and 2.2 shall be payable once only in the same proceedings. Fees 2.1 and 2.2 shall be payable as appropriate where the court allocates a case to a track for a trial of the assessment of damages. Fees 2.1 and 2.2 shall not be payable in relation in relation to a claim managed under a GLO after that GLO is made. Fee 2.1 shall not be payable where the procedure in Part 8 of the CPR is used. Fee 2.1 shall not be payable in proceedings where the only claim is a claim to recover a sum of money and the sum claimed does not exceed 1,000. Fee 2.2 shall not be payable in respect of a small claims hearing.	
2.3 Where permission to appeal is not required or has been granted by the lower court on filing an appellants notice, or, on filing a respondents notice where the respondent is	£50

appealing or wishes to ask the appeal court to uphold the order of the lower court for reasons different from or additional to those given by the lower court: (a) in relation to claims allocated to the small claims track	
(b) in relation to other claims Where in an appeal notice permission to appeal or an extension of time for appealing is applied for (or both are applied for) – • on filing an appellants notice, or, • where a respondent is appealing, on filing a respondents notice:	£100
(c) in relation to claims allocated to the small claims track	£100
(d) in relation to other claims Where fee 2.3(c) has been paid and permission to appeal (or extension of time) is not granted, 50 shall be refunded to the party who paid fee 2.3(c).	£150

2.4 On an application on notice where no other fee is specified	£50
2.5 On an application by consent or without notice for a judgment or order where no other fee is specified. For the purpose of fee 2.5 a request for a judgment or order on admission or in default shall not constitute an application and no fee shall be payable. Fee 2.5 shall not be payable on an application made under paragraph 8(3) of Schedule 6 to the Road Traffic Act 1991. *Fees 2.4 and 2.5* Fees 2.4 and 2.5 shall not be payable when an application is made in an appeal notice or is filed at the same time as an appeal notice.	£25
2.6 On an application for a summons or order for a witness to attend court to be examined on oath or an order for evidence to be taken by deposition, other than an application for which fee 4.3 is payable	£30
2.7 On an application to vary a judgment or suspend enforcement (where more than one remedy is sought in the same application only one fee shall be payable)	£25

3. Determination of costs	
Transitional provision *Where a bill of costs or a request for detailed assessment or a request for a detailed assessment hearing is filed pursuant to an order made by the court before the coming into operation of this Order, or an application is made to the judge to review a taxation made before the coming into operation of this Order, the fees payable shall be those which applied immediately before this Order came into force.*	
3.1 On the filing of a request for detailed assessment where the party filing the request is legally aided or is funded by the LSC and no other party is ordered to pay the costs of the proceedings	£80
3.2 On the filing of a request for a detailed assessment hearing in any case where fee 3.1 does not apply; or on the filing of a request for a hearing date for the assessment of costs payable to a solicitor by his client pursuant to an order under Part III of the Solicitors Act 1974	£150
Where there is a combined party and party and legal aid, or a combined party and party and LSC, or a combined party	

and party and legal aid and LSC determination of costs, fee 3.2 shall be attributed proportionately to the party and party, legal aid, or LSC (as the case may be) portion of the bill on the basis of the amount allowed.	
3.3 On a request for the issue of a default costs certificate	£40
3.4 On an appeal against a decision made in detailed assessment proceedings or on a request or an application to set aside a default costs certificate	£50
3.5 On applying for the courts approval of a certificate of costs payable from the Community Legal Service Fund.	£20
Fee 3.5 is payable at the time of applying for approval and is recoverable only against the Community Legal Service Fund	
4. Enforcement	
4.1 On an application for or in relation to enforcement of a judgment or order of a county court or through a county court:	

in cases other than CCBC cases, by the issue of a warrant of execution against goods except a warrant to enforce payment of a fine;	(a) Where the amount for which the warrant issues does not exceed £125 . . . . £25 (b) Where the amount for which the warrant issues exceeds £125 . . . . £25
in CCBC cases, by the issue of a warrant of execution against goods except a warrant to enforce payment of a fine	(c) Where the amount for which the warrant issues does not exceed £125 . . . . £20 (d) Where the amount for which the warrant issues exceeds £125 . . . . £40
4.2 On a request for a further attempt at execution of a warrant at a new address following a notice of the reason for non-execution (except a further attempt following suspension and CCBC cases)	£20
4.3 On an application to question a judgment debtor or other person on oath in connection with enforcement of a judgment	£40
4.4 On an application for a garnishee order nisi or a charging order nisi, or the appointment of a receiver by way of equitable execution	£50

Fee 4.4 shall be payable in respect of each party against whom the order is sought.	
4.5 On an application for a judgment summons	£80
4.6 On the issue of a warrant of possession or a warrant of delivery	£80
Where the recovery of a sum of money is sought in addition, no further fee is payable.	
4.7 On an application for an attachment of earnings order (other than a consolidated attachment of earnings order) to secure payment of a judgment debt	£50
Fee 4.7 is payable for each defendant against whom an order is sought. Fee 4.7 is not payable where the attachment of earnings order is made on the hearing of a judgment summons.	
4.8 On a consolidated attachment of earnings order or on an administration order	for every £1 or part of a £1 of the money paid into court in respect of debts due to creditors......................10p

Fee 4.8 shall be calculated on any money paid into court under any order at the rate in force at the time when the order was made (or, where the order has been amended, at the time of the last amendment before the date of payment).	
4.9 On the application for the recovery of a tribunal award	£30
4.10 On a request for an order to recover an increased penalty charge provided for in a parking charge certificate issued under paragraph 6 of Schedule 6 to the Road Traffic Act 1991 or on a request for an order to recover amounts payable by a person other than a London authority under an adjudication of a parking adjudicator pursuant to section 73 of the Road Traffic Act 1991;	£5
on a request to issue a warrant of execution to enforce such an order	
Fee 4.10 is payable on a request for an order but no further fee is payable on a request to issue a warrant of execution.	
5. Sale	
5.1 For removing or taking steps to remove goods to a place of deposit	The reasonable expenses incurred

Fee 5.1 is to include the reasonable expenses of feeding and caring for any animals.	
5.2 For advertising a sale by public auction pursuant to section 97 of the County Courts Act 1984	The reasonable expenses incurred
5.3 For the appraisement of goods	5p in the £1 or part of a £1 of the appraised value
5.4 For the sale of goods (including advertisements, catalogues, sale and commission and delivery of goods)	15p in the £1 or part of a £1 on the amount realised by the sale or such other sum as the district judge may consider to be justified in the circumstances
5.5 Where no sale takes place by reason of an execution being withdrawn, satisfied or stopped	(a) 10p in the £1 or part of a £1 on the value of the goods seized, the value to be the appraised value where the goods have been appraised or such other sum as the district judge may consider to be justified in the circumstances; and in addition (b) any sum payable under fee 5.1, 5.2 or 5.3
6. Copy documents	
6.1 On a request for a copy of a document (other than where fee 6.2 applies):	
(a) for the first page (except the first page of a subsequent copy of the same document supplied at the same time)	£1

(b) per page in any other case	20p
Fee 6.1 shall be payable for a faxed copy or for examining a plain copy and marking it as an examined copy	
Fee 6.1 shall be payable whether or not the copy is issued as an office copy.	
6.2 On a request for a copy of a document required in connection with proceedings and supplied by the party making the request at the time of copying, for each page.	20p
6.3 On a request for a copy of a document on a computer disk or in other electronic form, for each such copy.	£3
7. Registry of County Court Judgments	
7.1 On a request for the issue of a certificate of satisfaction or on a request for cancellation of the entry of a judgment in the Register where the judgment is satisfied in full within one month of the date of its entry	£10
8. Companies Act 1985 and Insolvency Act 1986	
8.1 On entering a bankruptcy petition:	

(a) if presented by a debtor or the personal representative of a deceased debtor	£120
(b) if presented by a creditor or other person	£150
8.2 On entering a petition for an administration order	£100
8.3 On entering any other petition	£150
One fee only is payable where more than one petition is presented in relation to a partnership.	
8.4 (a) On a request for a certificate of discharge from bankruptcy	£50
(b) and after the first certificate, for each copy *Requests and applications with no fee* No fee is payable on a request or on an application to the court by the Official Receiver when applying only in the capacity of Official Receiver to the case (and not as trustee or liquidator), or on an application to set aside a statutory demand.	£1

Crown Copyright 2000